SRA
Open Court Reading

W9-AAM-647

Core Decodable Takehomes

Core Decodables 1–62

Grade 1

Book 1

Mc Graw Hill Education

Bothell, WA • Chicago, IL • Columbus, OH • New York, NY

MHEonline.com

Send all inquiries to:
McGraw-Hill Education
8787 Orion Place
Columbus, OH 43240

ISBN: 978-0-07-674530-2
MHID: 0-07-674530-9

Printed in the United States of America.

1 2 3 4 5 6 7 8 9 QVS 20 19 18 17 16 15 14

Contents

About the Decodable Takehomes

The **SRA Open Court Reading** *Decodable Takehomes* allow your students to apply their knowledge of phonic elements to read simple, engaging texts. Each story supports instruction in a new phonic element and incorporates elements and words that have been learned earlier.

The students can fold and staple the pages of each *Decodable Takehome* to make books of their own to keep and read. We suggest that you keep extra sets of the stories in your classroom for the students to reread.

How to make a Takehome

1. Tear out the pages you need.

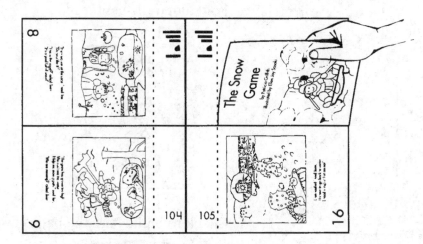

2. Place pages 4 and 5, and pages 2 and 7 faceup.

For 16-page book

3. Place the pages on top of each other in this order: pages 8 and 9, pages 6 and 11, pages 4 and 13, and pages 2 and 15.

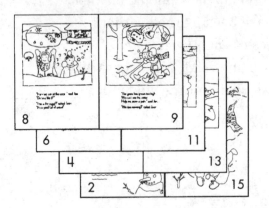

4. Fold along the center line.

5. Check to make sure the pages are in order.

6. Staple the pages along the fold.

For 8-page book

3. Place pages 4 and 5 on top of pages 2 and 7.

4. Fold along the center line.

5. Check to make sure the pages are in order.

6. Staple the pages along the fold.

Just to let you know...

A message from _____

Help your child discover the joy of independent reading with *SRA Open Court Reading.* From time to time your child will bring home his or her very own *Pre-Decodable* or *Decodable Takehomes* to share with you. With your help, these stories can give your child important reading practice and a joyful shared reading experience.

You may want to set aside a few minutes every evening to read these stories together. Here are some suggestions you may find helpful:

- Do not expect your child to read each story perfectly, but concentrate on sharing the book together.
- Participate by doing some of the reading.
- Talk about the stories you read, give lots of encouragement, and watch as your child becomes more fluent throughout the year!

Learning to read takes lots of practice. Sharing these stories is one way that your child can gain that valuable practice. Encourage your child to keep the *Pre-Decodable* or *Decodable Takehomes* in a special place. This collection will make a library of books that your child can read and reread. Take the time to listen to your child read from his or her library. Just a few moments of shared reading each day can give your child the confidence needed to excel in reading.

Children who read every day come to think of reading as a pleasant, natural part of life. One way to inspire your child to read is to show that reading is an important part of your life by letting him or her see you reading books, magazines, newspapers, or any other materials. Another good way to show that you value reading is to share a *Pre-Decodable* or *Decodable Takehome* with your child each day.

Successful reading experiences allow children to be proud of their newfound reading ability. Support your child with interest and enthusiasm about reading. You won't regret it!

High-Frequency Words

a	boy	from	I	now	sleep	was
about	brown	get	if	of	some	water
after	but	girl	in	old	take	way
all	by	go	into	on	that	we
am	call	going	is	one	the	well
an	came	good	it	or	their	went
and	can	got	its	out	them	were
any	come	green	jump	over	then	what
are	could	had	just	pretty	there	when
around	day	has	know	put	they	where
as	did	have	like	red	this	will
ask	do	he	little	ride	to	with
at	don't	help	long	right	too	would
away	down	her	look	said	two	yellow
be	every	here	make	saw	up	yes
before	five	him	me	see	very	you
big	for	his	my	she	walk	your
blue	four	how	no	six	want	

Sound/Spelling Correspondences in Core Decodables

1. Pre-decodable
2. Pre-decodable
3. Pre-decodable
4. Pre-decodable
5. Pre-decodable
6. /s/ spelled *s*, /m/ spelled *m*, /a/ spelled *a*
7. /t/ spelled *t, tt*
8. Review
9. /d/ spelled *d*
10. /n/ spelled *n*
11. /i/ spelled *i*
12. /h/ spelled *h_*
13. Review
14. /p/ spelled *p*
15. /l/ spelled *l, ll*
16. /o/ spelled *o*
17. /b/ spelled *b*
18. Review
19. /k/ spelled *c*
20. special spelling *al, all*
21. /k/ spelled *k, ■ck*
22. /r/ spelled *r*
23. Review
24. /f/ spelled *f, ff*
25. /s/ spelled *ss*
26. /g/ spelled *g*
27. /j/ spelled *j*
28. Review
29. /j/ spelled *■dge*
30. /u/ spelled *u*
31. /z/ spelled *z, zz*
32. /z/ spelled *_s*
33. Review
34. /ks/ spelled *■x*
35. /e/ spelled *e*
36. *-ed* ending: /ed/, /d/
37. *-ed* ending: /t/
38. Review
39. /e/ spelled *_ea_*
40. /sh/ spelled *sh*
41. /th/ spelled *th*
42. /ch/ spelled *ch, ■tch*
43. Review
44. /or/ spelled *or, ore*
45. /ar/ spelled *ar*
46. /w/ spelled *w_*
47. /w/ spelled *wh_*
48. Review
49. /er/ spelled *er, ir*
50. /er/ spelled *ur*
51. /er/ spelled *ear*
52. /ng/ spelled *■ng*
53. Review
54. Schwa
55. *-le, -el, -il, -al*
56. /nk/ spelled *■nk*
57. /kw/ spelled *qu_*
58. Review
59. /y/ spelled *y_*
60. /v/ spelled *v*
61. /ā/ spelled *a, a_e*
62. Review
63. /ī/ spelled *i, i_e*
64. /s/ spelled *ce, ci_*
65. /j/ spelled *ge, gi_*
66. Review
67. /ō/ spelled *o, o_e*
68. /ū/ spelled *u, u_e*
69. Review
70. /ē/ spelled *e, e_e*
71. /ē/ spelled *ee, ea*
72. Review /ē/
73. /ē/ spelled *_y, _ie_*
74. /ē/ spelled *_ey*
75. Review
76. /s/ spelled *cy*
77. /ā/ spelled *ai_, _ay*
78. Review
79. /ī/ spelled *_igh*
80. /ī/ spelled *_y, _ie*
81. Review /ī/
82. /ō/ spelled *oa_, _ow*
83. /ū/ spelled *_ew, _ue*
84. Review
85. /m/ spelled *_mb*
86. /n/ spelled *kn_, gn*
87. /r/ spelled *wr_*
88. /f/ spelled *ph*
89. Review
90. /ōō/ spelled *oo*
91. /ōō/ spelled *u, _ue*
92. Review
93. /ōō/ spelled *_ew, u_e*
94. /oo/ spelled *oo*
95. Review
96. /ow/ spelled *ow*
97. /ow/ spelled *ou_*
98. /aw/ spelled *au_, aw*
99. Review
100. /aw/ spelled *augh, ough*
101. /oi/ spelled *oi, _oy*
102. Review
103. Prefixes *un-, dis-*
104. Prefixes *im-, in-, re-*
105. Review /ā/ and /a/
106. Review /ī/ and /i/
107. Review /ō/ and /o/
108. Review /ū/ and /u/
109. Review /ē/ and /e/
110. Review consonant digraphs
111. Review r-controlled vowels
112. Review /oo/ and /ōō/
113. Review diphthongs
114. Review inflectional endings

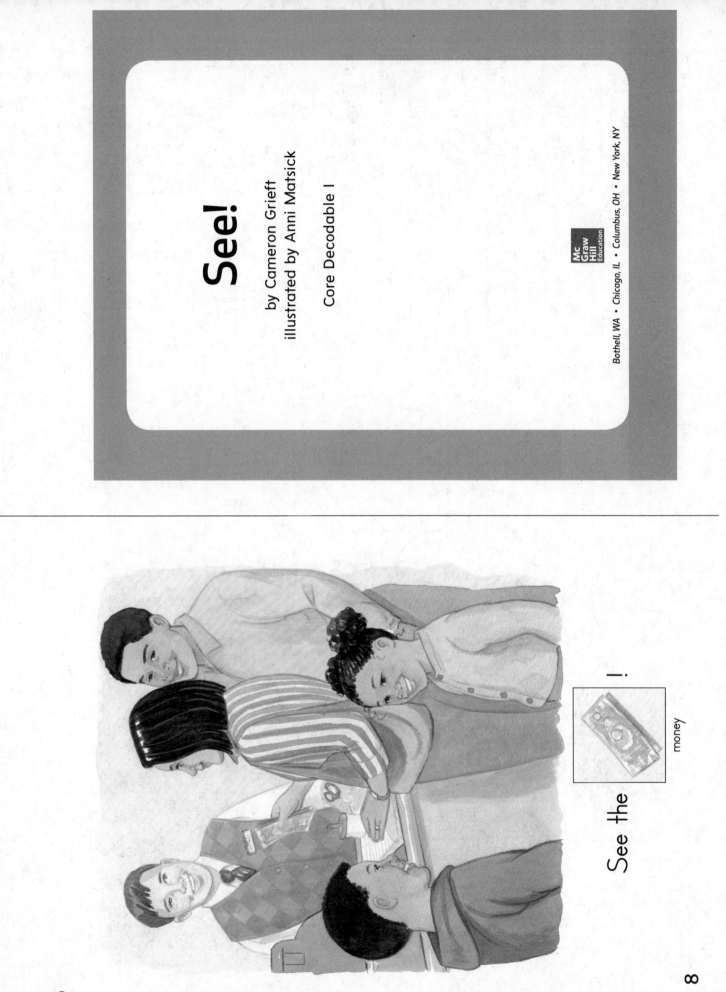

See!

by Cameron Grieft

illustrated by Anni Matsick

Core Decodable 1

Mc Graw Hill Education

Bothell, WA • Chicago, IL • Columbus, OH • New York, NY

See the ▢ !

money

9

8

2

See the 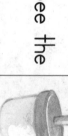.

paste

7

10

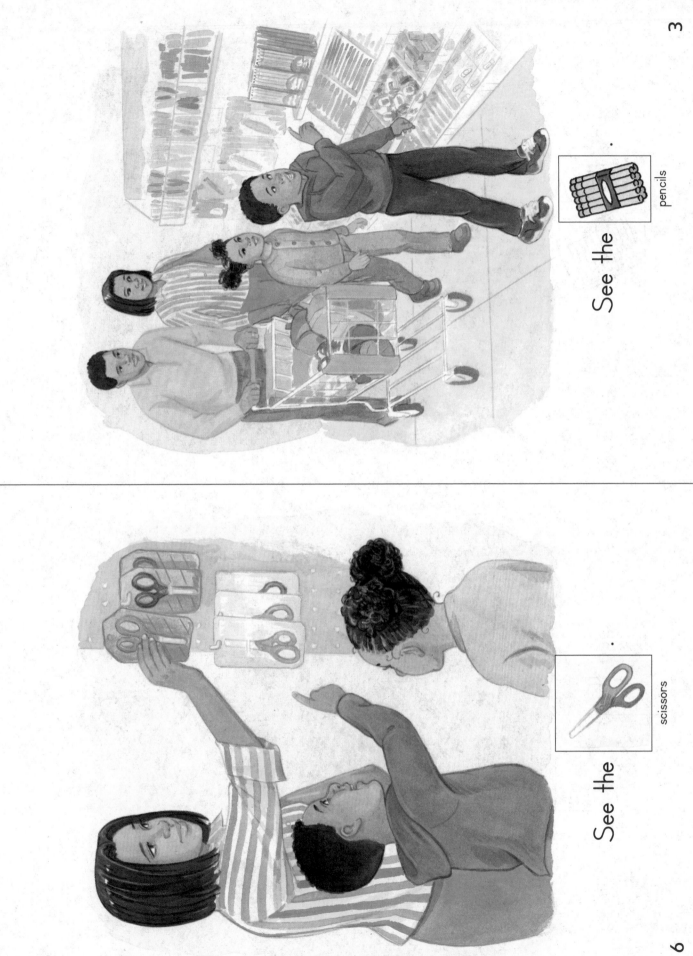

See the .

pencils

11

See the .

scissors

See the

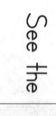

paper

.

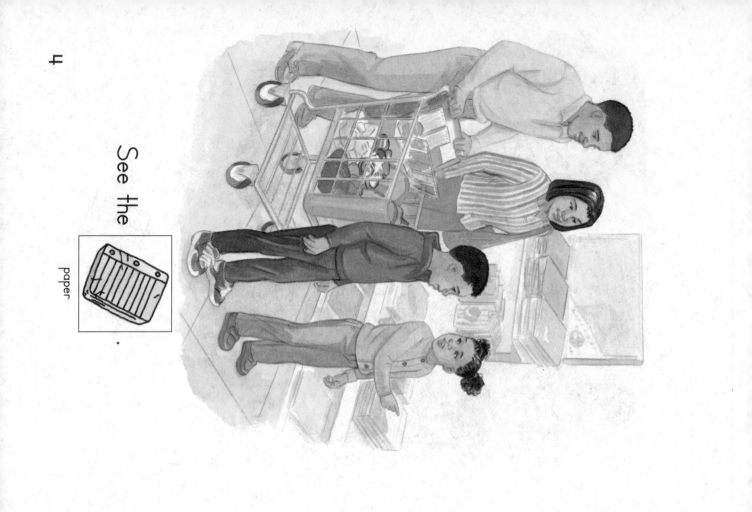

See the

crayons

.

Up

by Tameron Dennis

illustrated by Eva Vagreti

Core Decodable 2

Mc Graw Hill Education

Bothell, WA • Chicago, IL • Columbus, OH • New York, NY

The  is up!

boy

MHEonline.com

Send all inquiries to:
McGraw-Hill Education
8787 Orion Place
Columbus, OH 43240

See the  !

clock

14

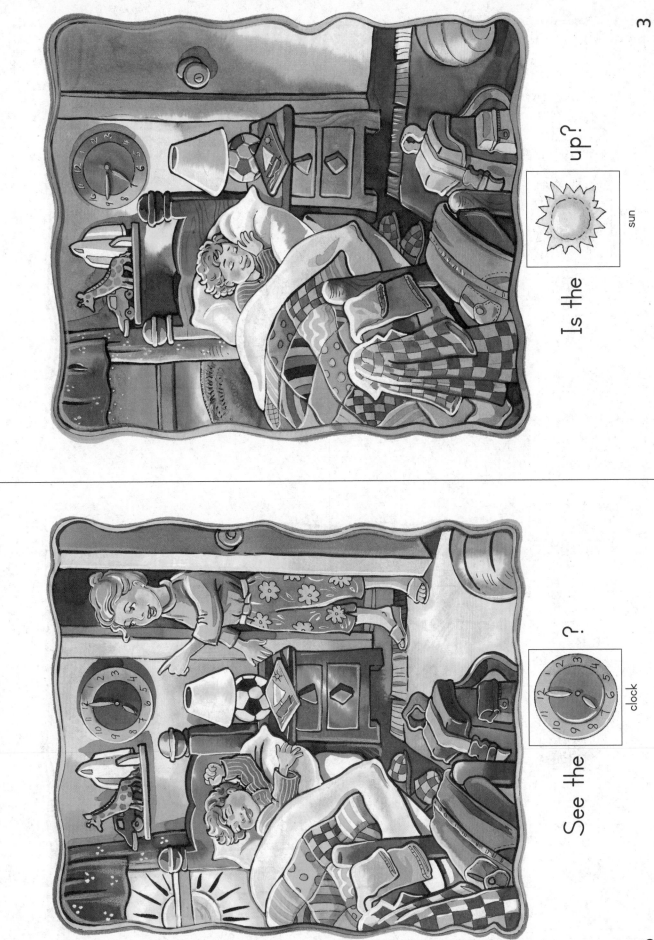

Is the up?

sun

3

See the ?

clock

6

15

The  is up.

sun

Is the  up?

boy

I Have

by Cameron Grieft

illustrated by Eva Vagreti

Core Decodable 3

Mc Graw Hill Education

Bothell, WA • Chicago, IL • Columbus, OH • New York, NY

I have

jam

2

I have

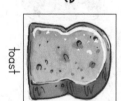
toast

.

7

18

I have ____ .

cereal

I have ____ .

orange juice

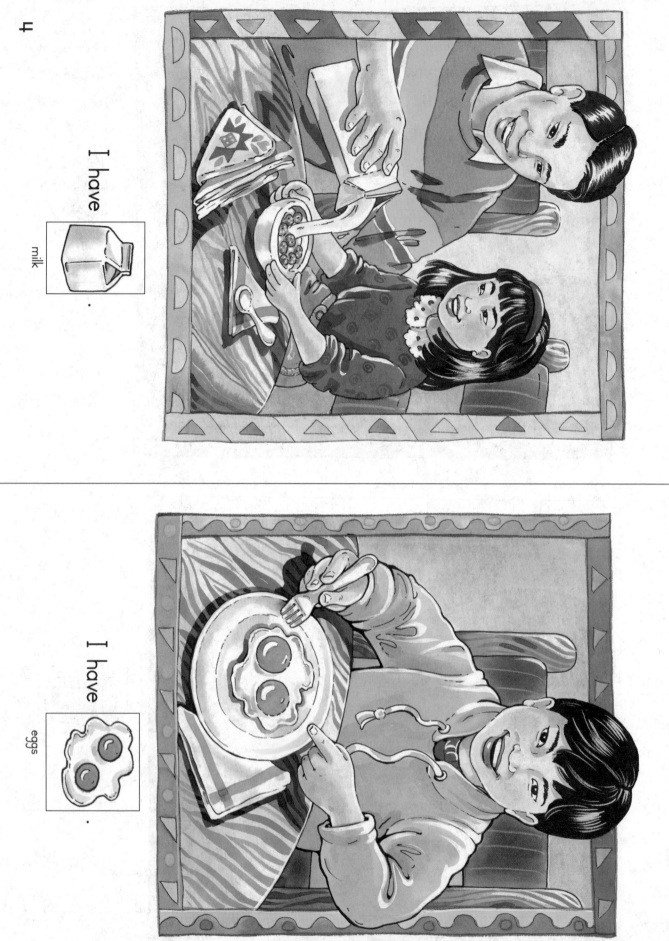

I have _____ .

milk

I have _____ .

eggs

There Is

by Tameron Dennis

illustrated by Eva Vagreti

Core Decodable 4

Mc Graw Hill Education

Bothell, WA • Chicago, IL • Columbus, OH • New York, NY

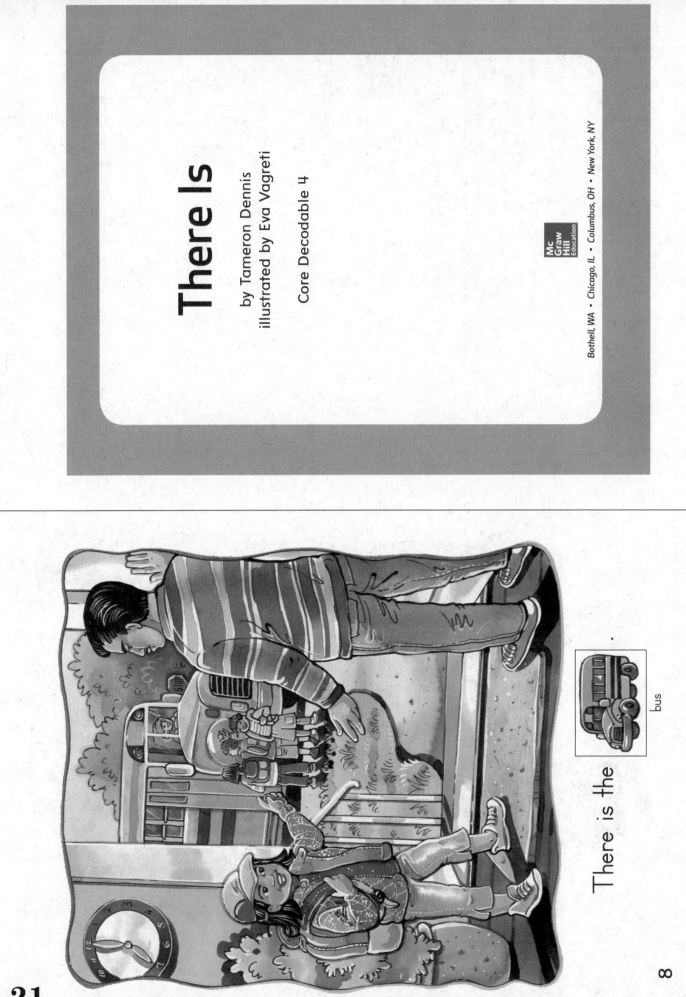

There is the ___.

bus

2

There is a

book

.

7

22

There is a  .

jacket

There is a .

lunchbox

There is a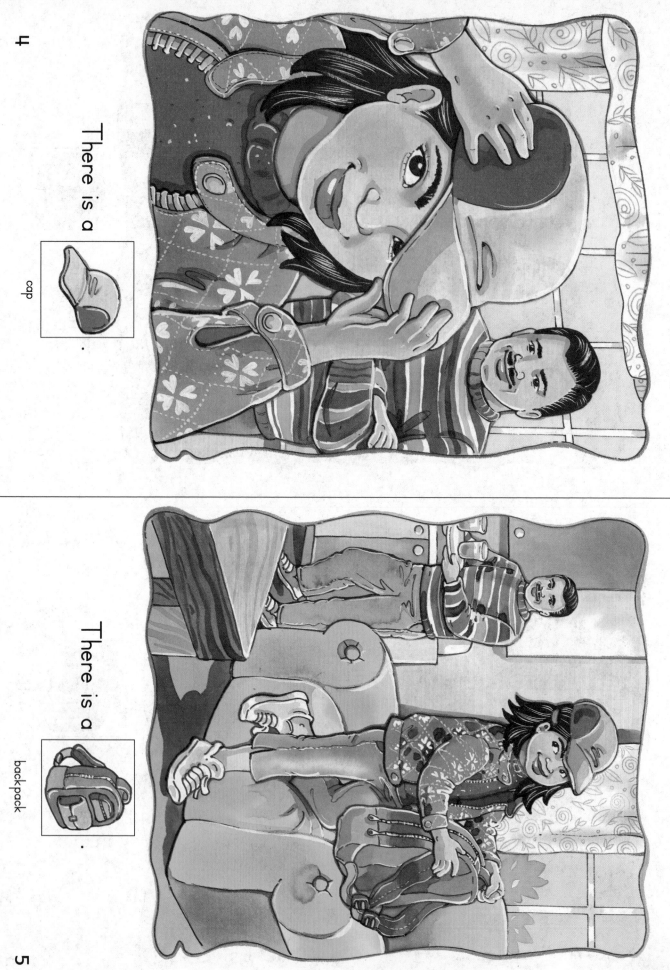

cap

.

There is a

backpack

.

I Can See

by Cameron Grieft

illustrated by Eva Vagreti

Core Decodable 5

Mc Graw Hill Education

Bothell, WA • Chicago, IL • Columbus, OH • New York, NY

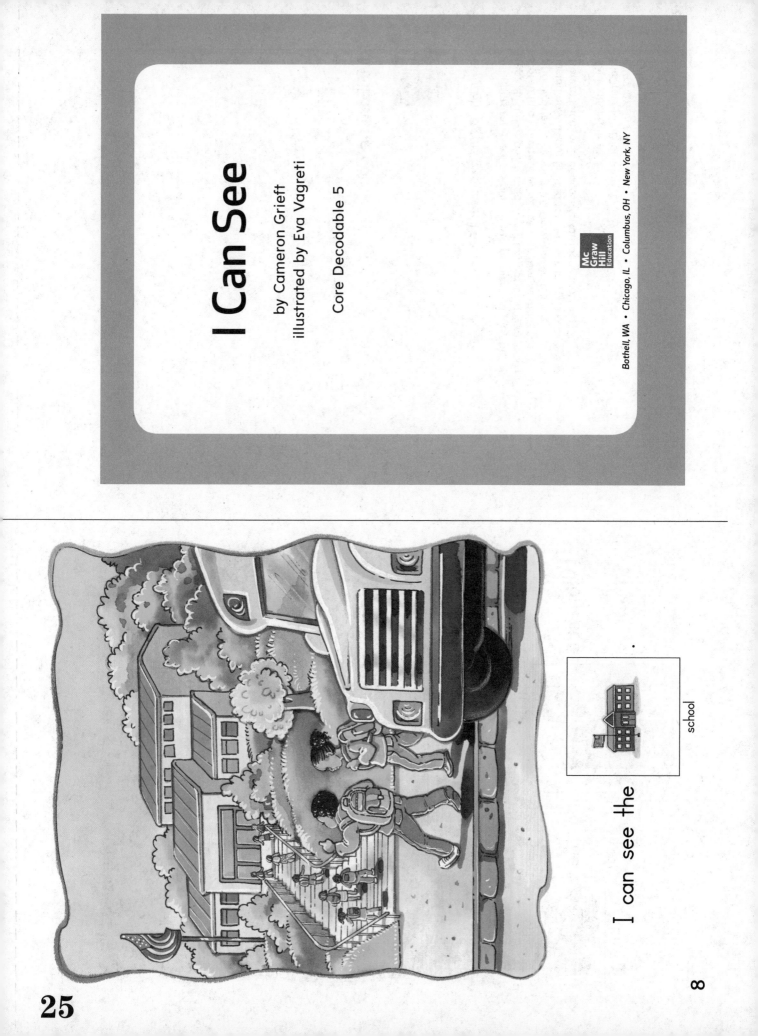

I can see the .

school

I can see

girls

on the

bus

.

I can see the

bus

I can see

boys

on the

bus

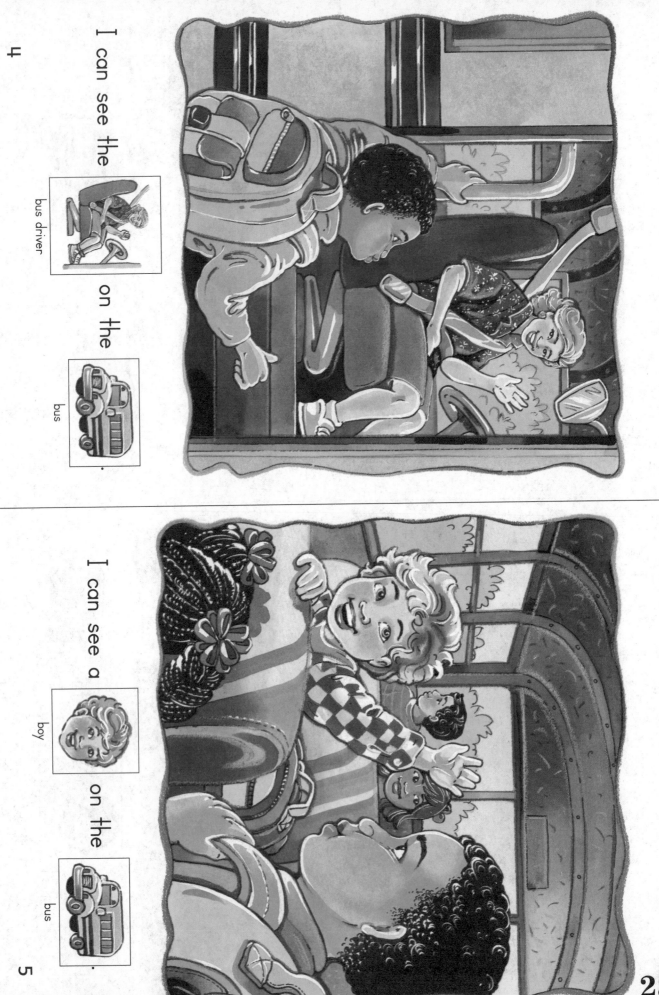

I can see the on the .

bus driver

bus

4

I can see a on the .

boy

bus

5

Sam, Sam, Sam

by Linda Cave
illustrated by Meryl Henderson

Core Decodable 6

Mc Graw Hill Education

Bothell, WA • Chicago, IL • Columbus, OH • New York, NY

I am Sam.

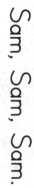
2

Sam, Sam, Sam.

7

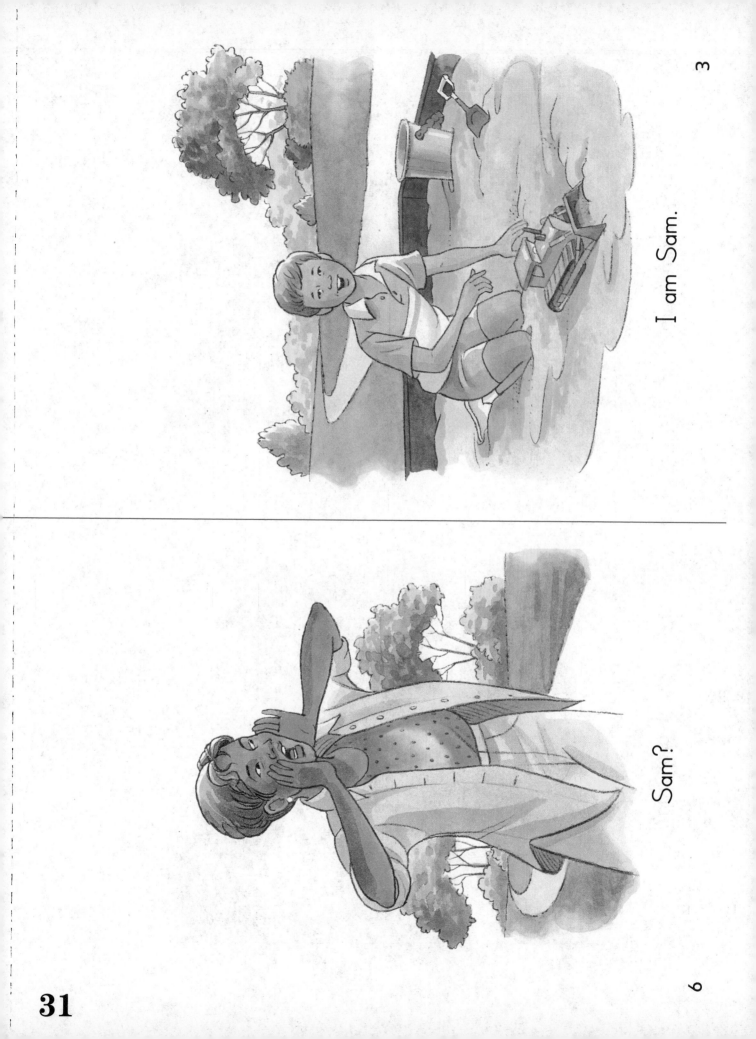

I am Sam.

Sam?

I am Sam.

I am Sam.

Matt and Sam

by Martha Wood

illustrated by Olivia Cole

Core Decodable 7

Mc Graw Hill Education

Bothell, WA • Chicago, IL • Columbus, OH • New York, NY

33

Sam and Matt sat.

8

MHEonline.com

Copyright © 2015 McGraw-Hill Education

All rights reserved. No part of this publication may be reproduced or distributed in any form or by any means, or stored in a database or retrieval system, without the prior written consent of McGraw-Hill Education, including, but not limited to, network storage or transmission, or broadcast for distance learning.

Send all inquiries to:
McGraw-Hill Education
8787 Orion Place
Columbus, OH 43240

2

Sam sat.

7

34

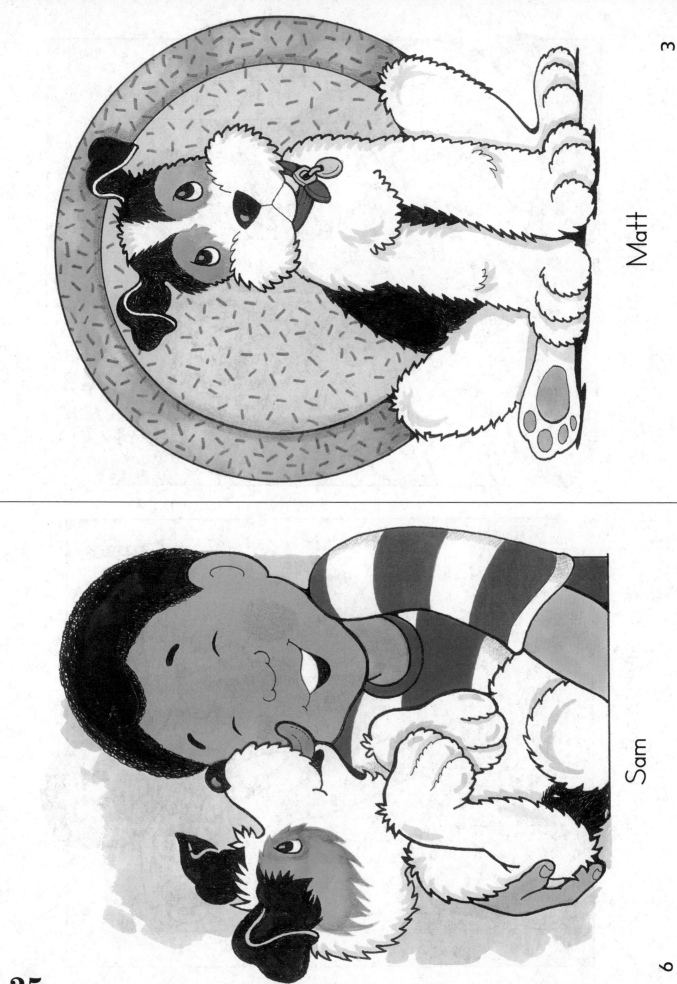

Matt

3

Sam

6

35

Matt sat.

Matt sat on Sam.

4

5

On a Mat

by Tameron Dennis
illustrated by Mark Corcoran

Core Decodable 8

Bothell, WA • Chicago, IL • Columbus, OH • New York, NY

Mc Graw Hill Education

I sat on a mat.

16

37

Tam sat. Sam sat. Matt sat.

Tam

Tam sat on a mat.

39

Tam on a mat

4

Tam sat.

13

40

Sam

5

I sat on Matt.

12

41

Sam on a mat

Matt sat on Sam.

Matt

Sam sat on Tam.

Matt on a mat

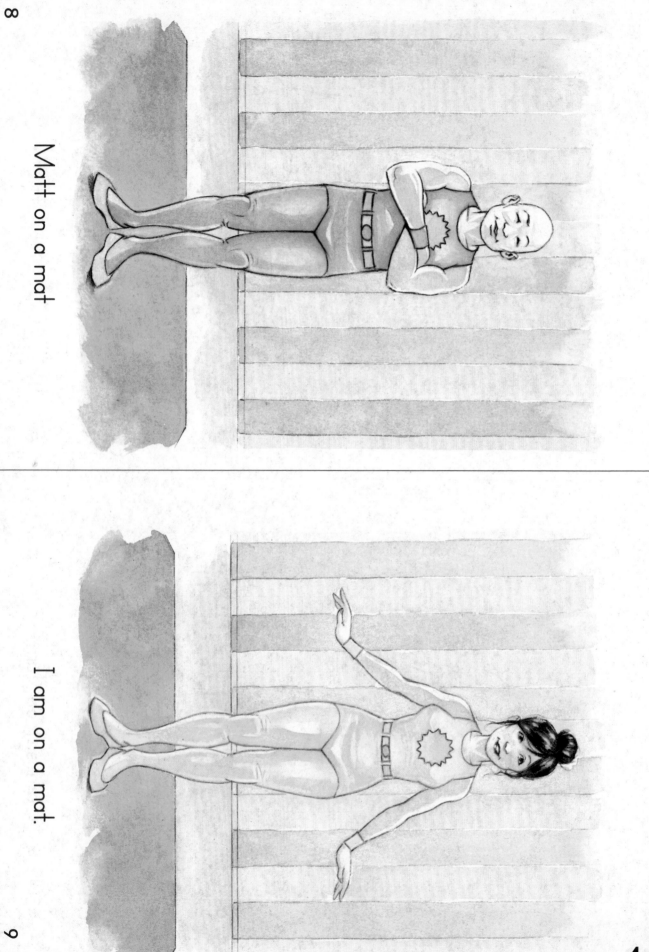

I am on a mat.

Dad Sat

by Tamera Williams

illustrated by Anni Matsick

Core Decodable 9

Mc Graw Hill Education

Bothell, WA • Chicago, IL • Columbus, OH • New York, NY

45

Tad, Tam, and Dad sat.

8

MHEonline.com

Copyright © 2015 McGraw-Hill Education

All rights reserved. No part of this publication may be reproduced or distributed in any form or by any means, or stored in a database or retrieval system, without the prior written consent of McGraw-Hill Education, including, but not limited to, network storage or transmission, or broadcast for distance learning.

Send all inquiries to:
McGraw-Hill Education
8787 Orion Place
Columbus, OH 43240

2

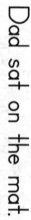

Dad sat on the mat.

7

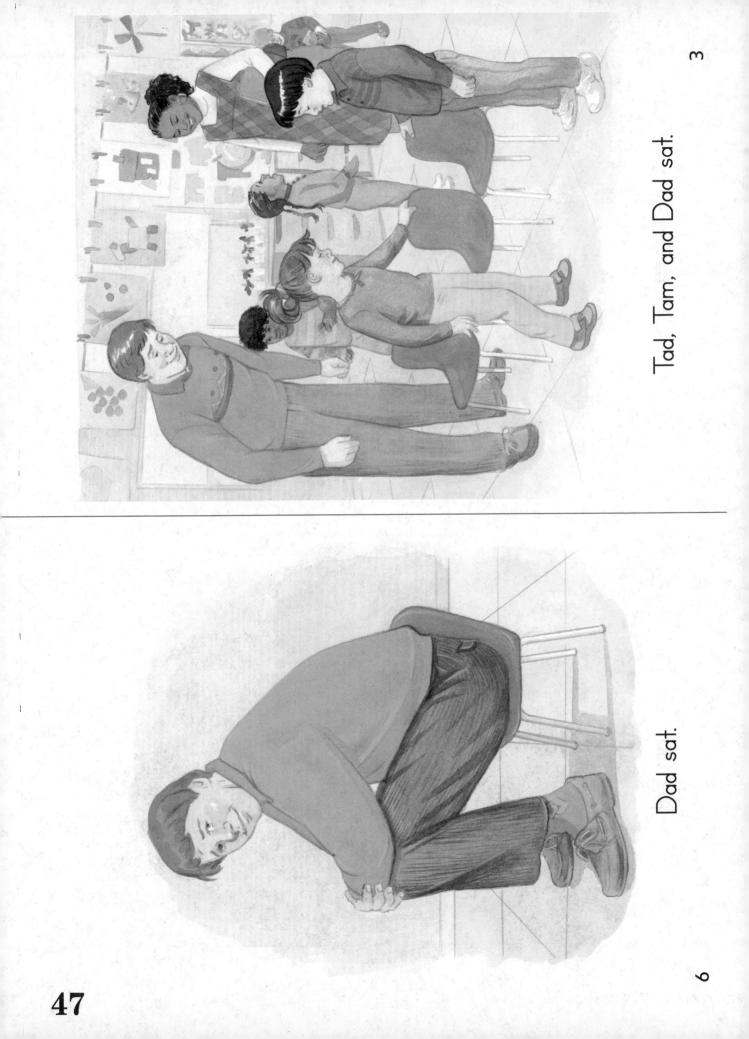

Tad, Tam, and Dad sat.

3

Dad sat.

47

6

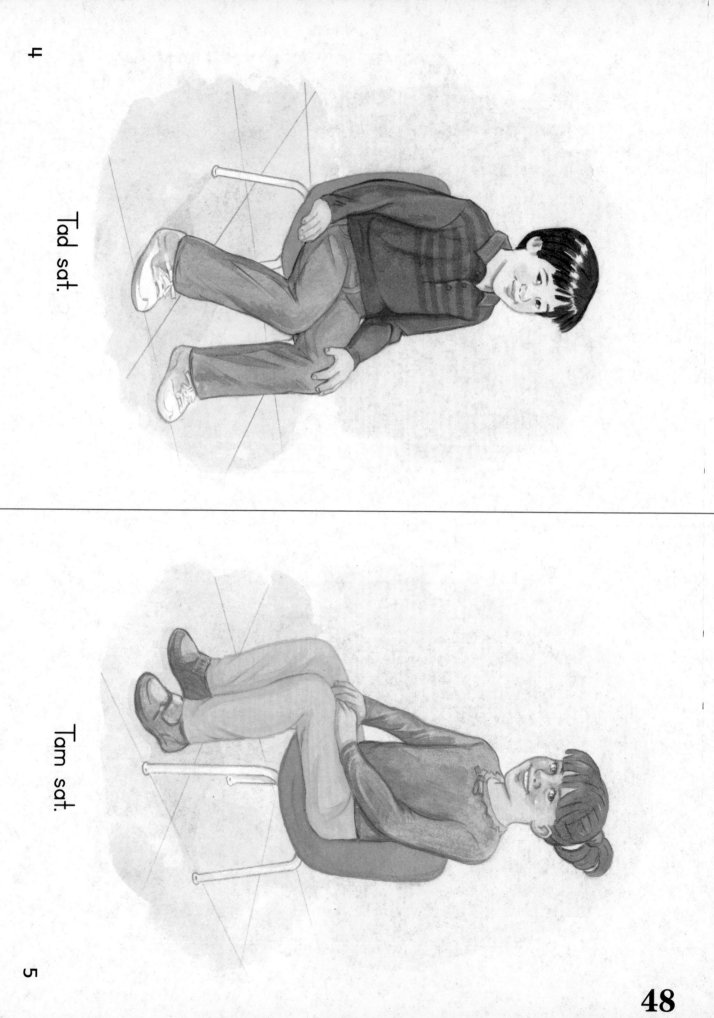

Tad sat.

Tam sat.

Ants

by Nancy Tyler
illustrated by Steve Henry

Core Decodable 10

McGraw Hill Education

Bothell, WA · Chicago, IL · Columbus, OH · New York, NY

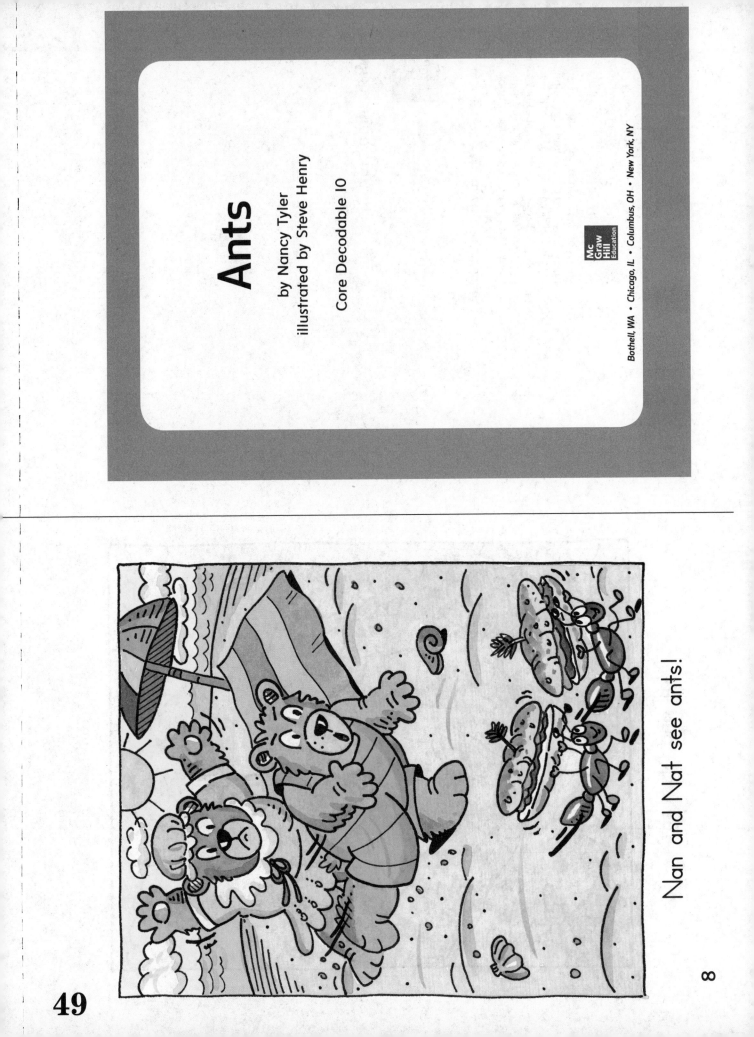

Nan and Nat see ants!

8

49

2

Nat and Nan sat.

7

51

Nat and Nan sat.

3

Ants see Nat and Nan.

6

Nat and Nan stand.

Nat and Nan stand and stand.

Sit

by Cecilia Winters
illustrated by Kate Flanagan

Core Decodable II

Mc Graw Hill Education

Bothell, WA • Chicago, IL • Columbus, OH • New York, NY

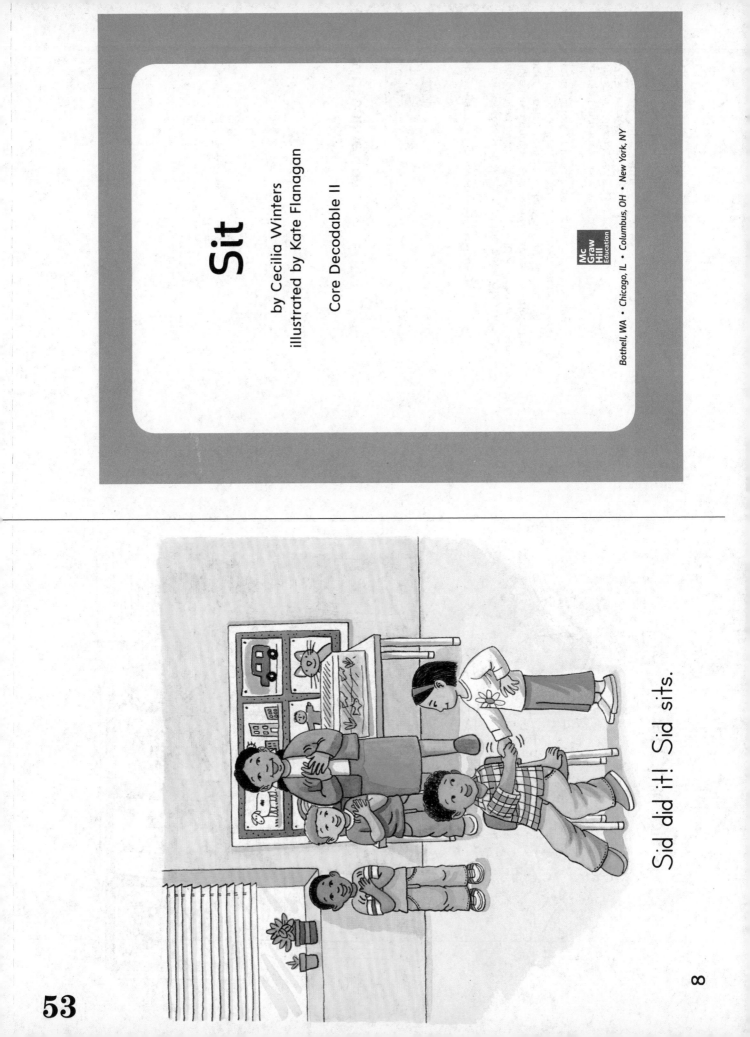

Sid did it! Sid sits.

8

Did Sid sit? Did Sis sit?

55

Sid, Sis, and Tim sit.

Did Tim sit? See Tim stand.

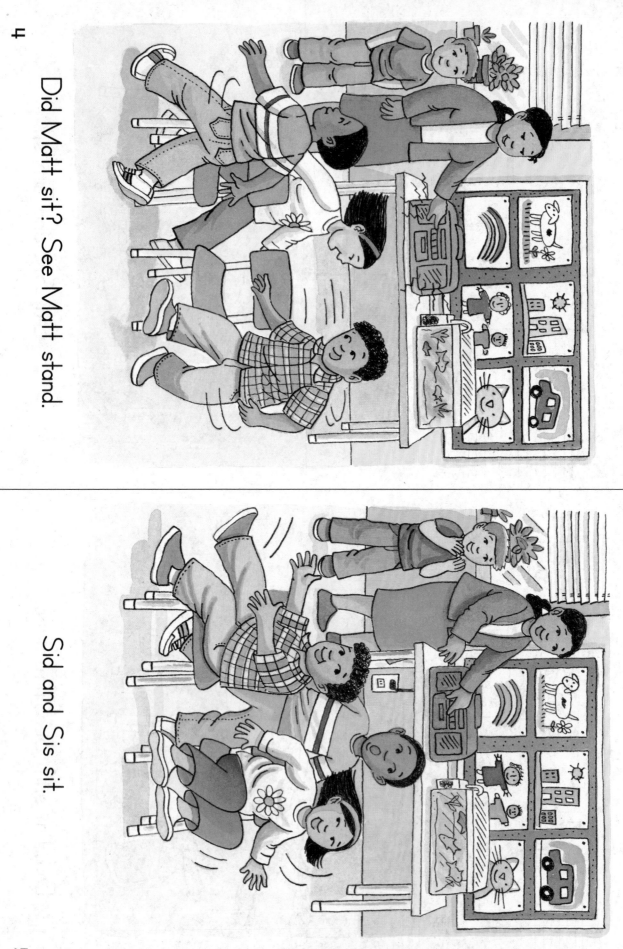

Did Matt sit? See Matt stand.

Sid and Sis sit.

A Hint

by Sidney Allen

illustrated by Kate Flanagan

Core Decodable 12

Mc Graw Hill Education

Bothell, WA • Chicago, IL • Columbus, OH • New York, NY

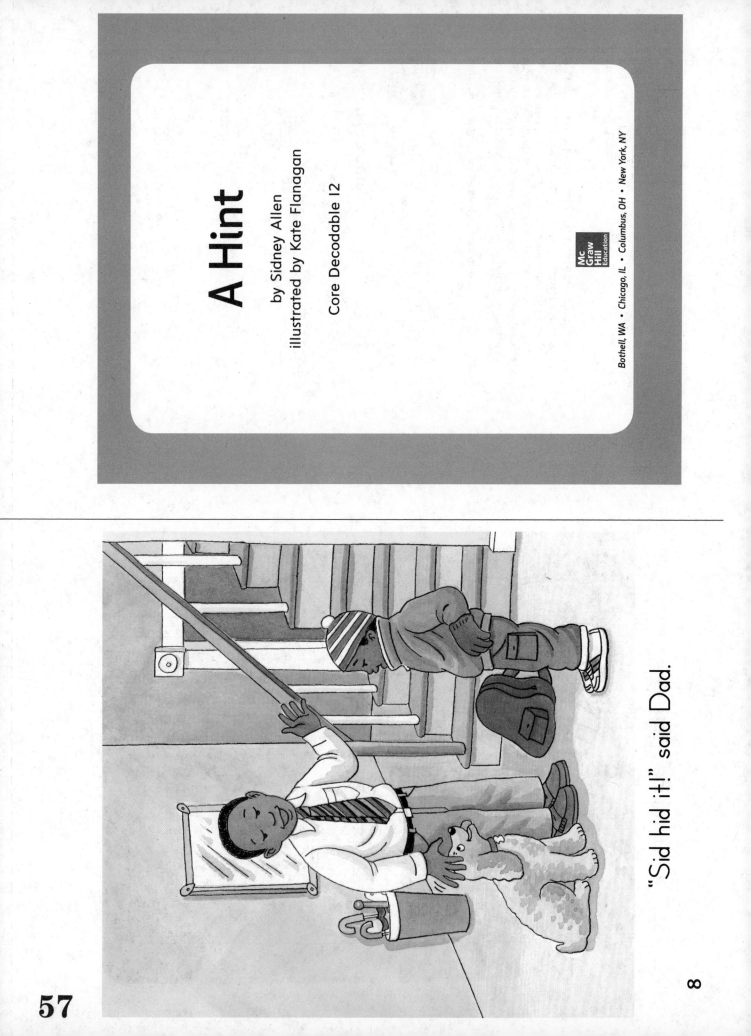

"Sid hid it!" said Dad.

8

57

MHEonline.com

Copyright © 2015 McGraw-Hill Education

All rights reserved. No part of this publication may be reproduced or distributed in any form or by any means, or stored in a database or retrieval system, without the prior written consent of McGraw-Hill Education, including, but not limited to, network storage or transmission, or broadcast for distance learning.

Send all inquiries to:
McGraw-Hill Education
8787 Orion Place
Columbus, OH 43240

2

"A hat!" said Tim.

7

58

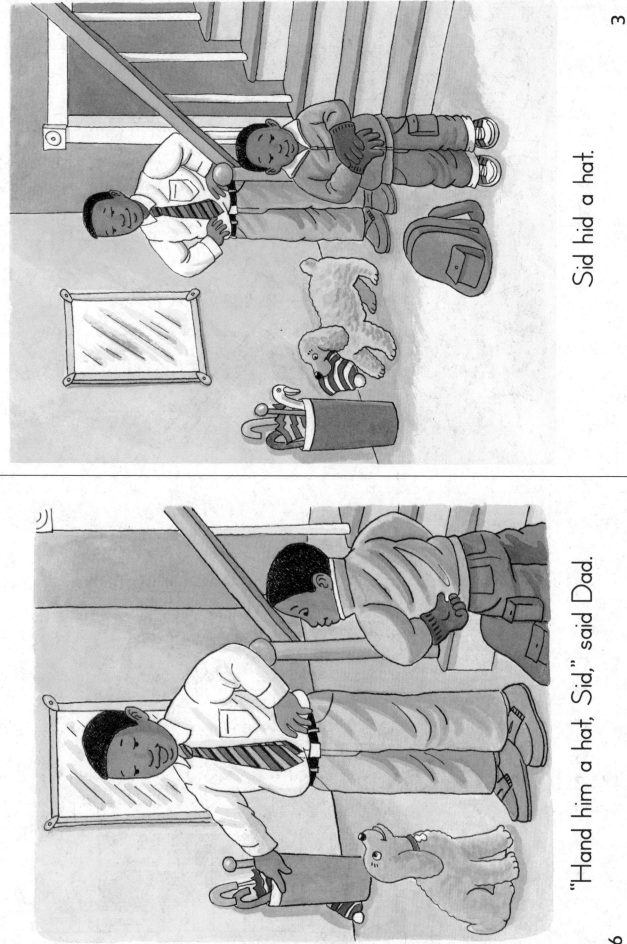

Sid hid a hat.

"Hand him a hat, Sid," said Dad.

"I had a hat," said Tim.

4

Dad had a hint.

5

Mints

by Tameron Dennis
illustrated by Kate Flanagan

Core Decodable 13

Mc Graw Hill Education

Bothell, WA • Chicago, IL • Columbus, OH • New York, NY

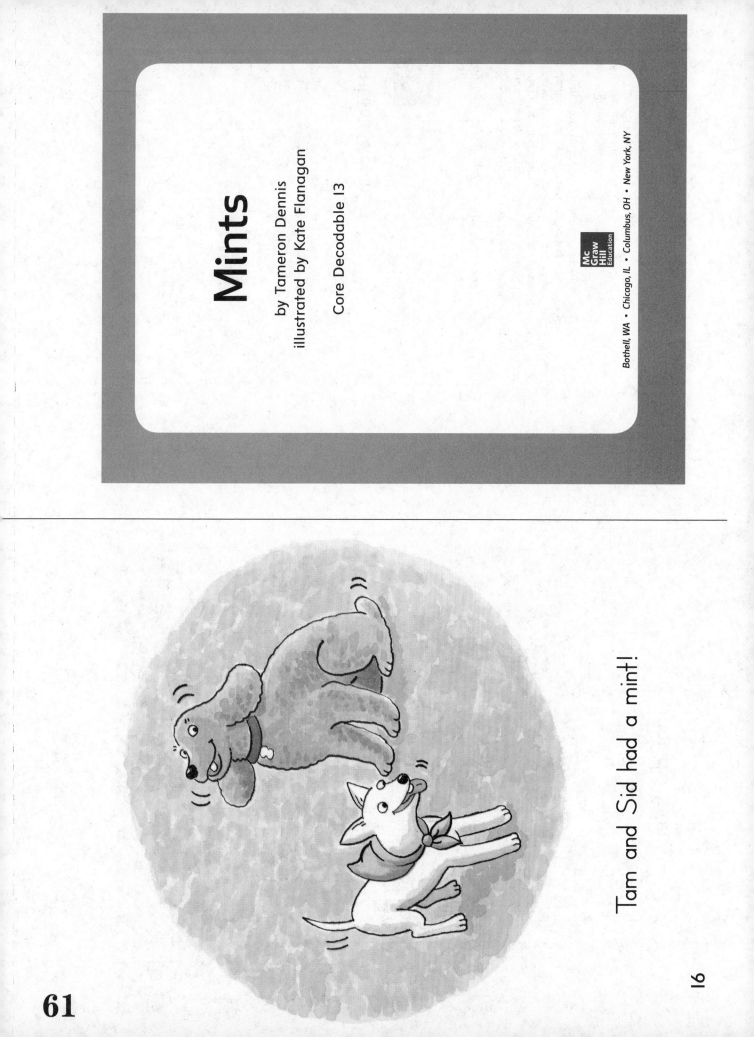

Tam and Sid had a mint!

16

61

2

Tam did stand.

15

Tim had a tin can.

"Stand, Tam," said Tim.

3

4

The tin can had mints in it.

Did Tam see it?

Tim had a mint.

5

Tim hid it in a hand.

12

65

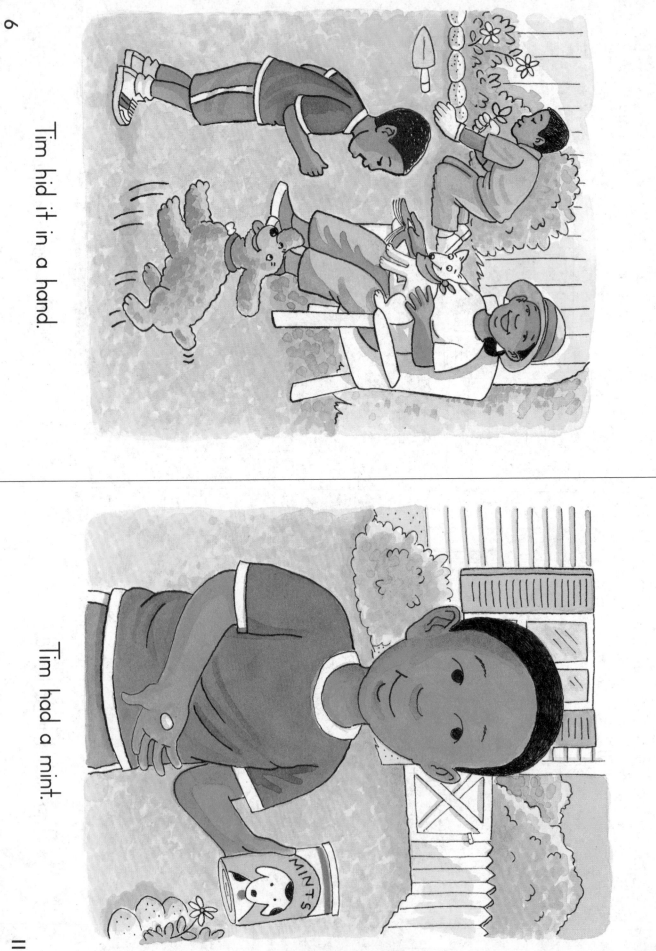

Tim hid it in a hand.

6

Tim had a mint.

11

67

Sid had a mint!

Did Sid see it?

"Sit, Sid," said Tim.

Sid sat.

Pat's Map

by Lucy Shepard
illustrated by Olivia Cole

Core Decodable 14

Mc Graw Hill Education

Bothell, WA • Chicago, IL • Columbus, OH • New York, NY

Sam nips Pat's map!

2

Sam hits Pat's map.

7

Pat's map sits on a mat.

3

Sam taps Pat's map.

6

71

4

Pat taps the map.

TAP TAP.

5

Sam stamps on Pat's map.

Lin and Hal

by Linda Johnson

illustrated by Paige Keiser

Core Decodable 15

Mc Graw Hill Education

Bothell, WA • Chicago, IL • Columbus, OH • New York, NY

73

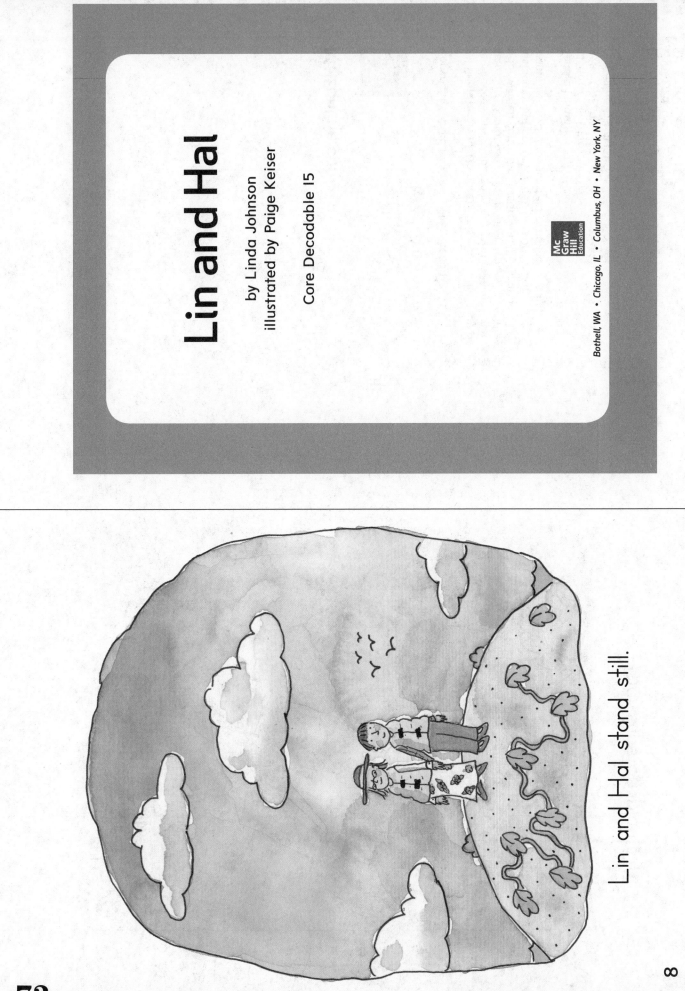

Lin and Hal stand still.

8

Hal slips on plants.

Lin had a plan.

3

Lin sits on a hill.

6

Hal can land in sand.

Lin slips in the sand.

A Spot

by Lucy Shepard

iillustrated by Olivia Cole

Core Decodable 16

Mc Graw Hill Education

Bothell, WA • Chicago, IL • Columbus, OH • New York, NY

Mom pats a spot.

8

77

2

Dad mops a spot.

7

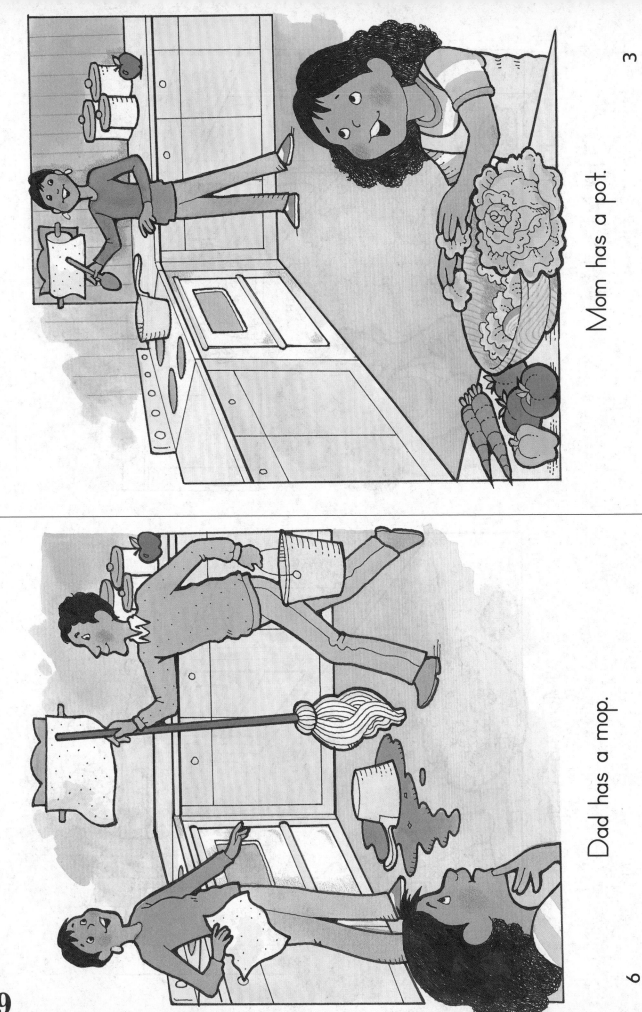

Mom has a pot.

Dad has a mop.

Mom has a hot pot.
The hot pot tips!

4

Mom has a spot.

5

Bob at Bat

by Nicole Michael

illustrated by Len Epstein

Core Decodable 17

Mc Graw Hill Education

Bothell, WA • Chicago, IL • Columbus, OH • New York, NY

Bob pants and pants.

8

81

MHEonline.com

Mc Graw Hill Education

Send all inquiries to:
McGraw-Hill Education
8787 Orion Place
Columbus, OH 43240

Bob bats. Bam!
Bob has a hit!

82

Bob is at bat.

3

Bob can stand and nod.

6

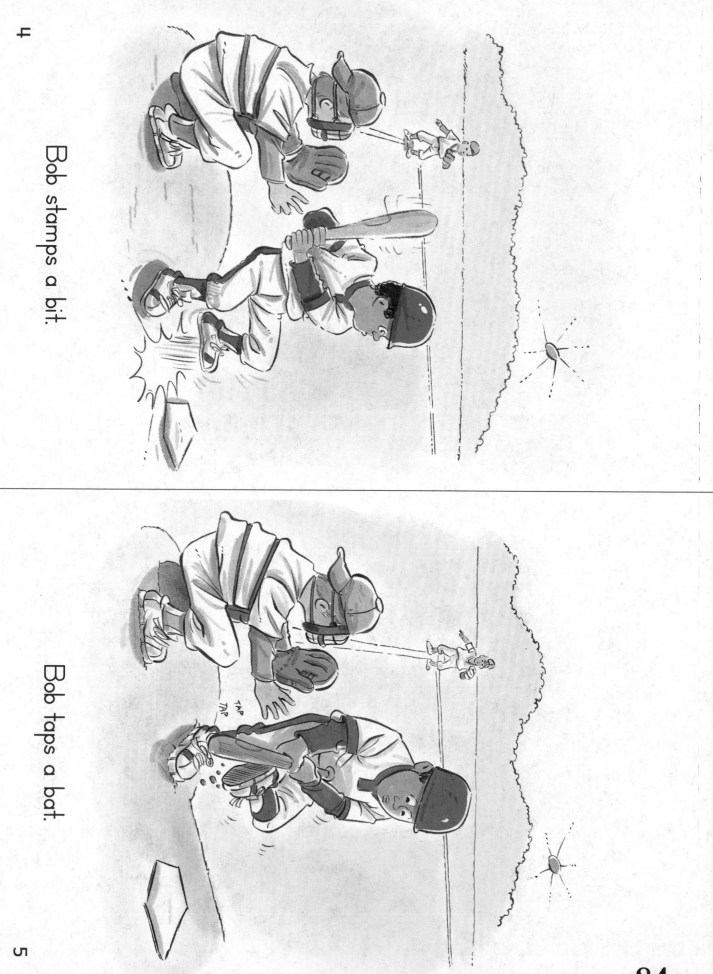

4

Bob stamps a bit.

5

Bob taps a bat.

Bill

by Tamera Williams

illustrated by Laura Logan

Core Decodable 18

Mc Graw Hill Education

Bothell, WA • Chicago, IL • Columbus, OH • New York, NY

"I can hop, spin, and tap!"

16

85

2

"I am not hot!" said Bill.

15

Pam and Bob hop past Bill.

3

"I am hot, hot, hot!" said Bill.

14

87

Bill did not hop.

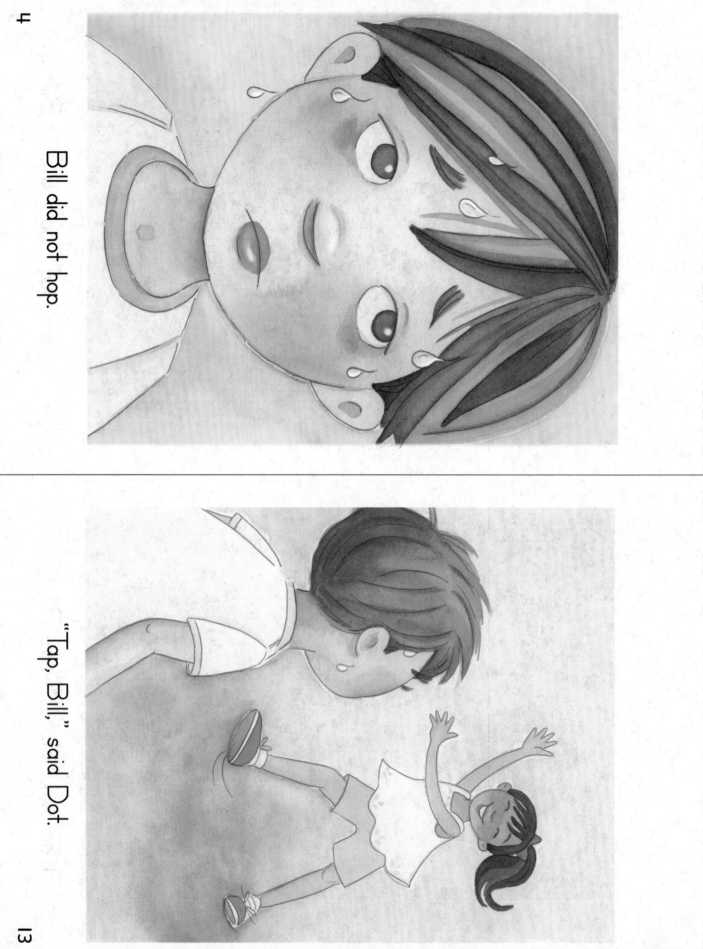

"Tap, Bill," said Dot.

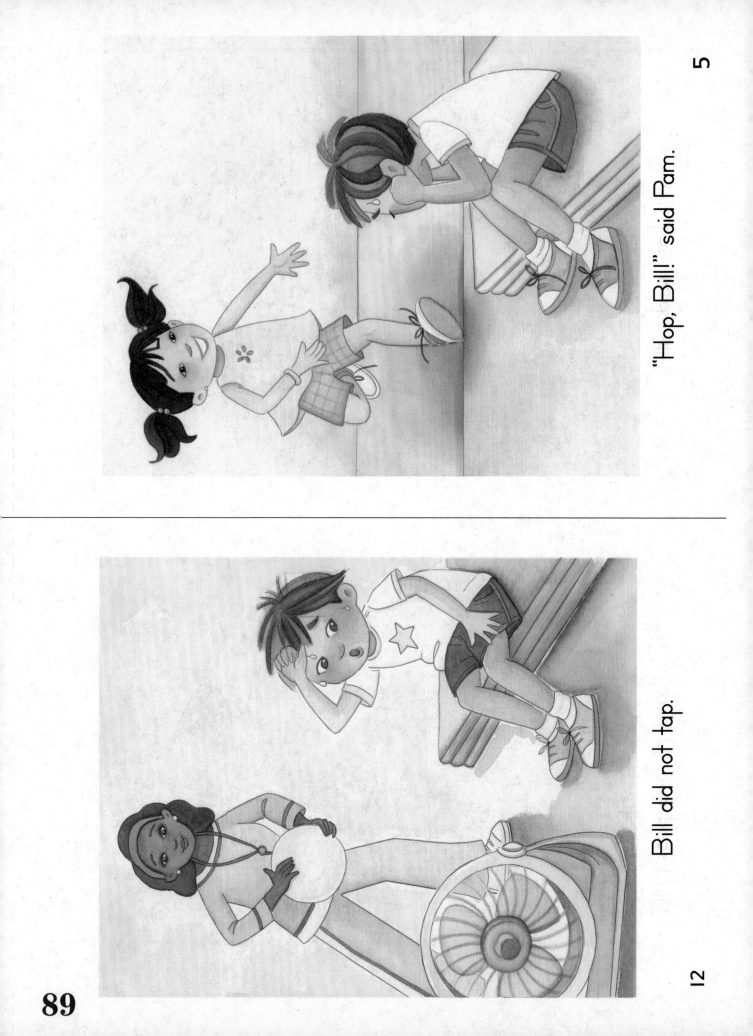

"Hop, Bill!" said Pam.

5

Bill did not tap.

12

89

"I am hot," said Bill.

6

Dot and Al tap past Bill.

11

90

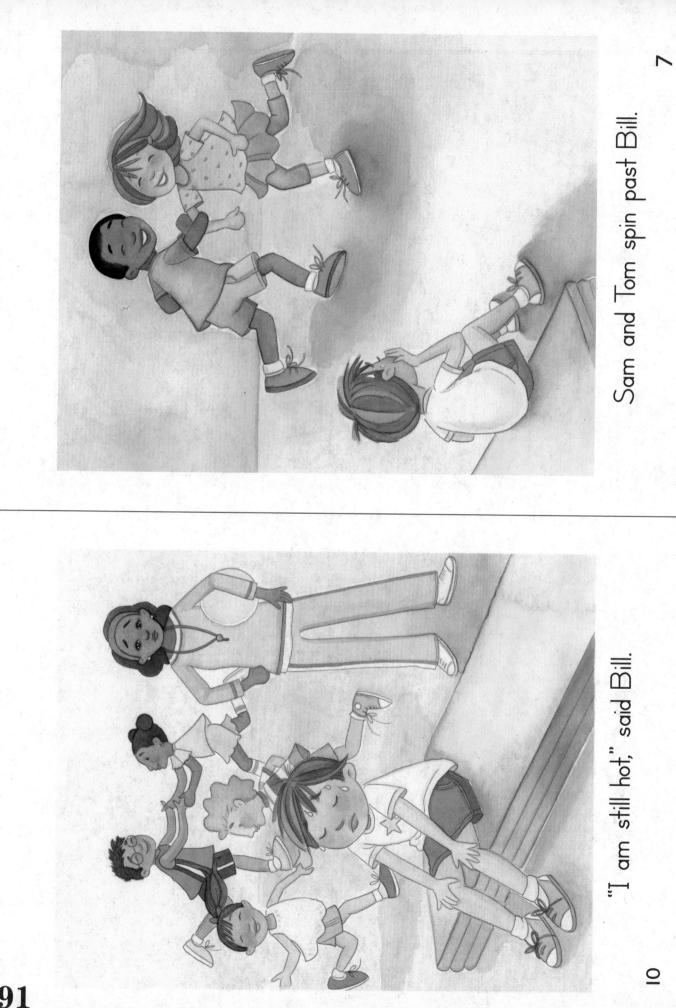

Sam and Tom spin past Bill.

7

"I am still hot," said Bill.

10

Bill did not spin.

"Spin, Bill," said Sam.

Nat's Cap

by Andrew Lunn
illustrated by Len Epstein

Core Decodable 19

Mc Graw Hill Education

Bothell, WA • Chicago, IL • Columbus, OH • New York, NY

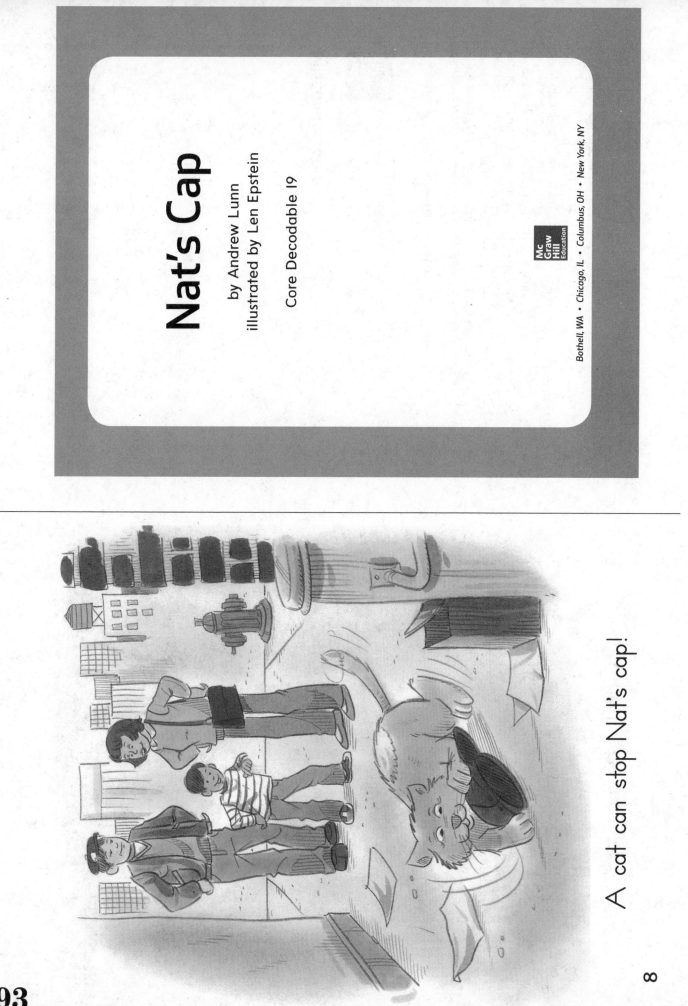

A cat can stop Nat's cap!

8

2

Can Nat's cap stop?

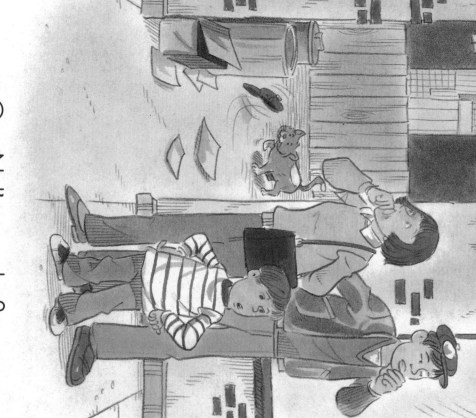

7

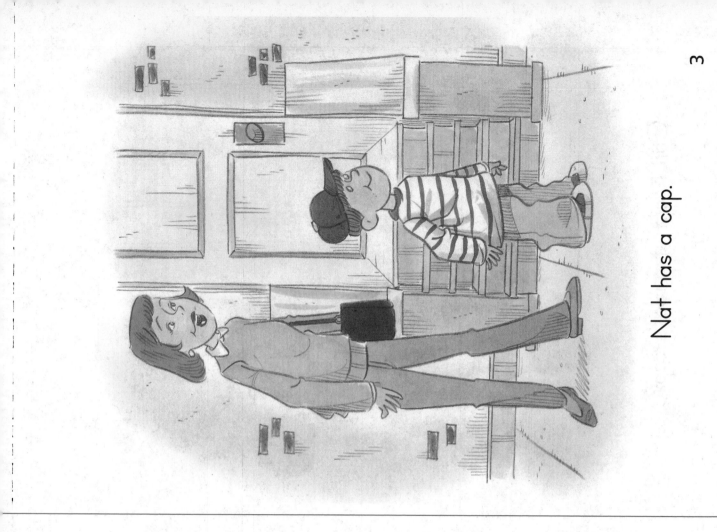

Nat has a cap.

A cab can't stop Nat's cap.

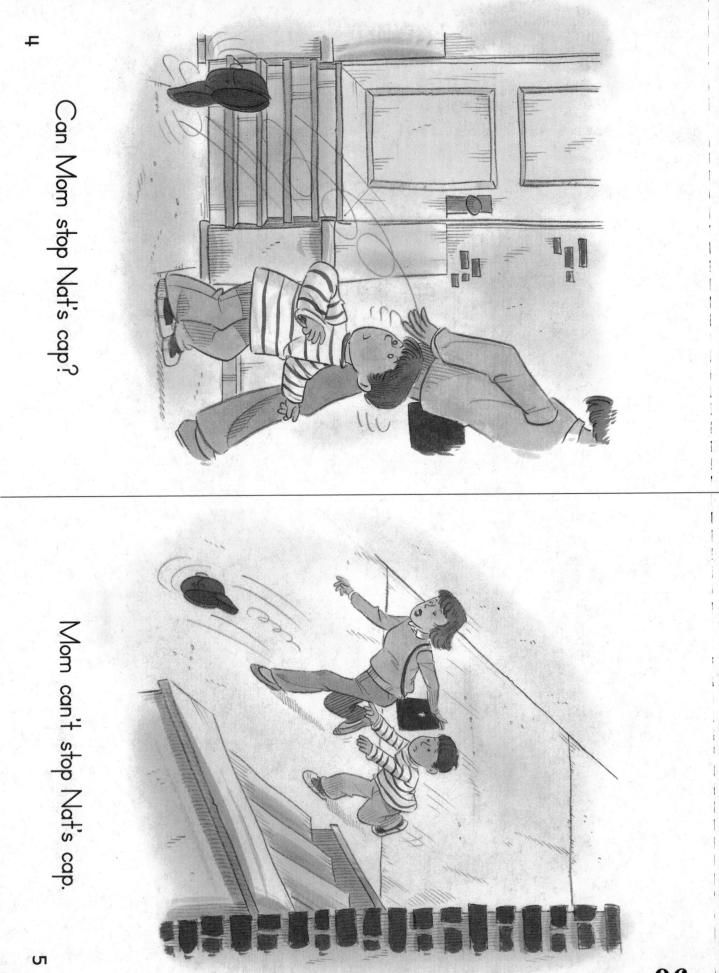

4

Can Mom stop Nat's cap?

Mom can't stop Nat's cap.

5

96

At the Mall

by Kimberly Irving
illustrated by Meryl Henderson

Core Decodable 20

Mc Graw Hill Education

Bothell, WA • Chicago, IL • Columbus, OH • New York, NY

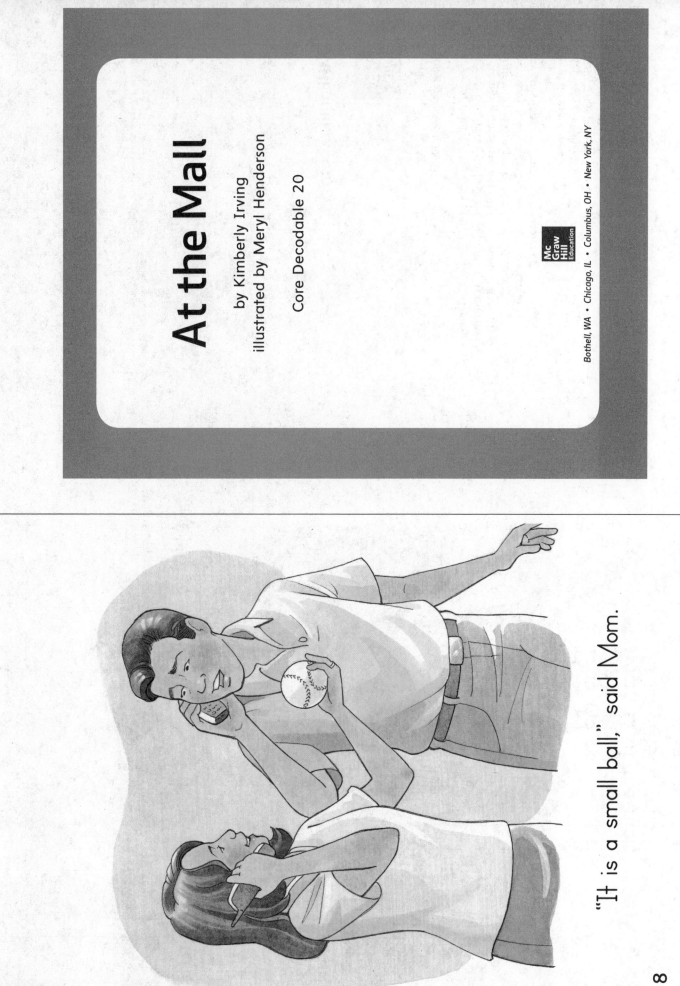

"It is a small ball," said Mom.

2

Dad did call.
Mom is at the mall!

7

98

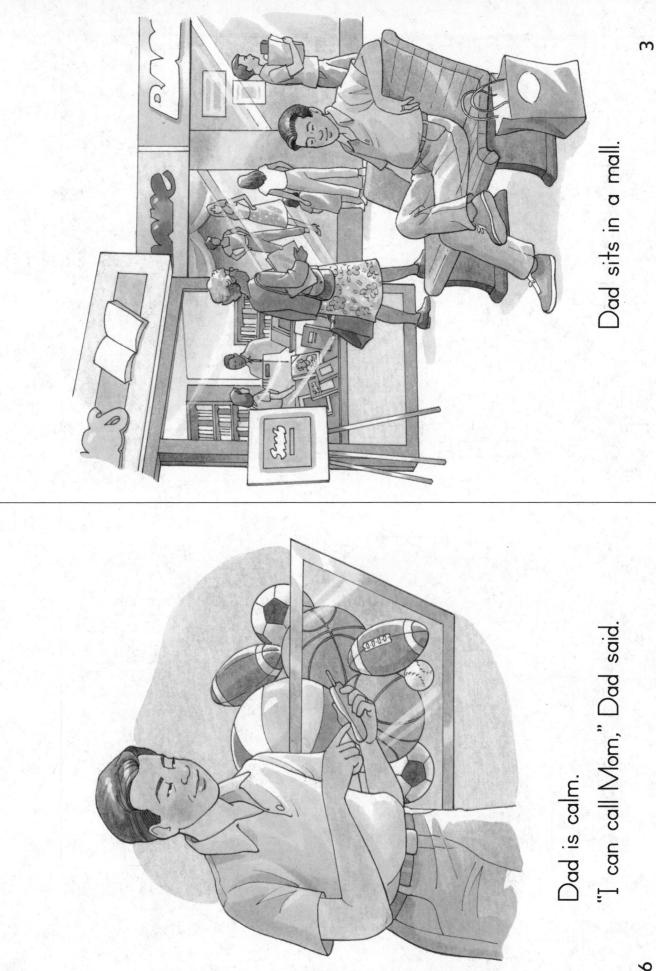

Dad sits in a mall.

3

Dad is calm.
"I can call Mom," Dad said.

6

Dad has a list.

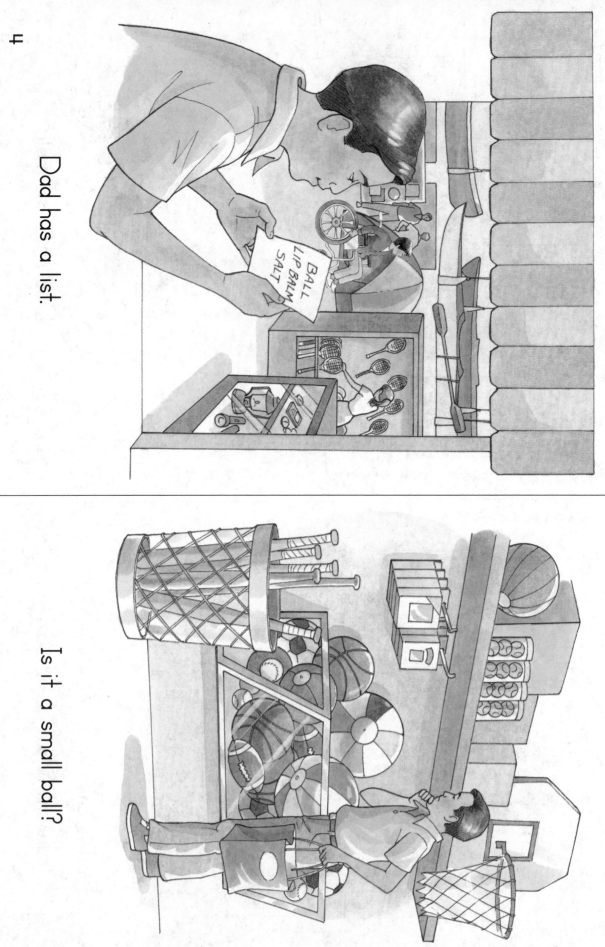

BALL
LIP BALM
SALT

Is it a small ball?

Picnic

by Pam Matthews

illustrated by Olivia Cole

Core Decodable 21

Mc Graw Hill Education

Bothell, WA • Chicago, IL • Columbus, OH • New York, NY

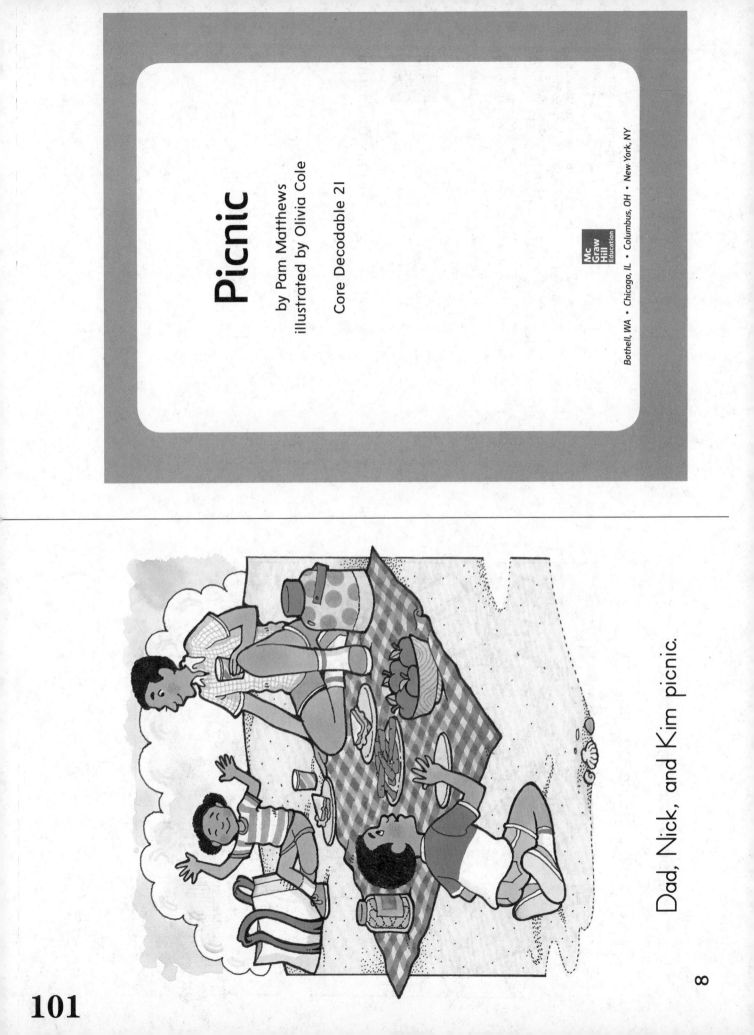

Dad, Nick, and Kim picnic.

8

2

Kim has the picnic sack.
Kim has milk and snacks.

7

102

Dad can pick snacks.

Dad and Nick stand.

Kim skips in the sand.

4

Nick can pack maps.

Kim sits in the back.

5

Rick and Rob

by Rich White
illustrated by Kersti Frigell

Core Decodable 22

McGraw Hill Education

Bothell, WA • Chicago, IL • Columbus, OH • New York, NY

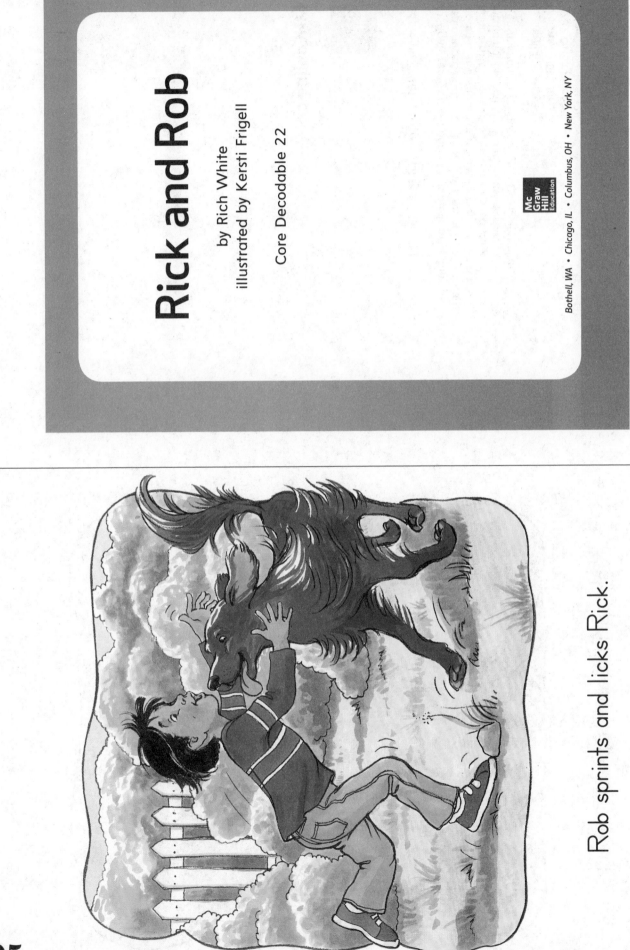

Rob sprints and licks Rick.

8

2

Rick sprints and trips on a rock.

7

106

Rick sits and prints.

3

Rob licks Rick. Rick can't pick a trick.

6

4

Rob licks Rick. Rick can't print.

Rick sits and picks a trick.

5

Cal and Kip

by Alex Yu

illustrated by Kersti Frigell

Core Decodable 23

Mc Graw Hill Education

Bothell, WA • Chicago, IL • Columbus, OH • New York, NY

109

The tall man trots past Cal and Kip.

16

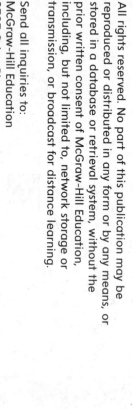

"It's hot," said Cal.

"Sip and drip a lot," said Kip.

110

A tall man is on the sand.

The tall man had a sip.

Bobcats spot the tall man.
Cal and Kip Bobcat talk.

4

"And Bobcats skip snacks," said Kip.

13

112

"The sand is hot," said Kip.

5

The tall man had a small snack.

12

113

The tall man sat on a small rock.

"Bobcats can't have backpacks," said Cal.

115

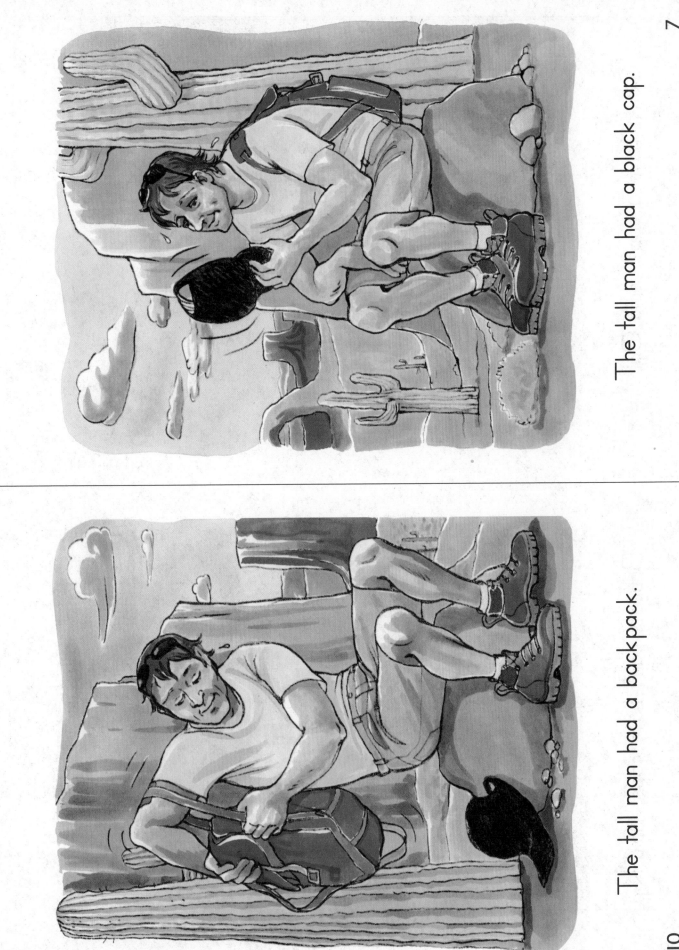

The tall man had a backpack.

The tall man had a black cap.

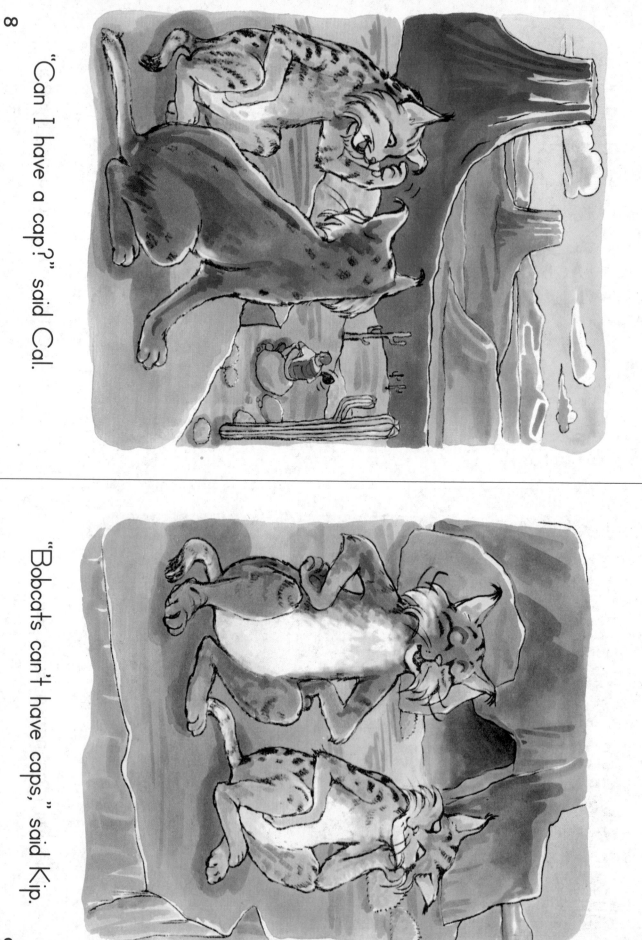

"Can I have a cap?" said Cal.

"Bobcats can't have caps," said Kip.

Bobcat

by Robert Bridges

illustrated by Meryl Henderson

Core Decodable 24

Mc
Graw
Hill
Education

Bothell, WA • Chicago, IL • Columbus, OH • New York, NY

A bobcat sprints fast!

117

8

Look! A bobcat can stand stiff.

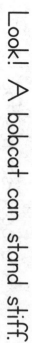

Look! A bobcat is on a cliff.
It sits on a flat rock.

3

A bobcat can look fast.

119

6

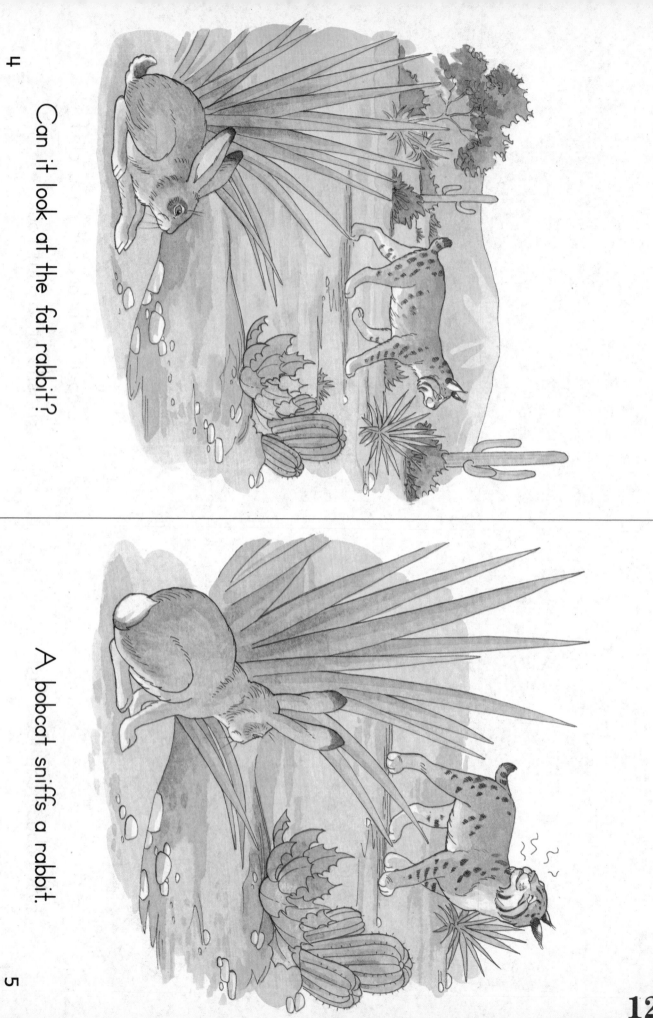

4

Can it look at the fat rabbit?

A bobcat sniffs a rabbit.

5

Pat's Class Trip

by Jessica Evans

illustrated by Meryl Henderson

Core Decodable 25

Mc Graw Hill Education

Bothell, WA • Chicago, IL • Columbus, OH • New York, NY

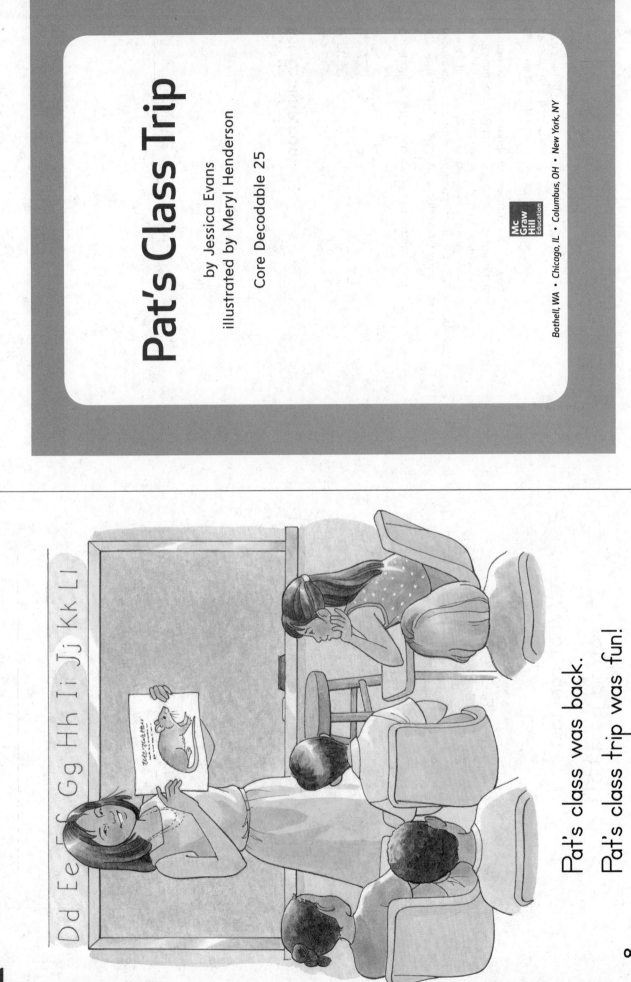

Dd Ee Ff Gg Hh Ii Jj Kk Ll

Pat's class was back.

Pat's class trip was fun!

MHEonline.com

Copyright © 2015 McGraw-Hill Education

Send all inquiries to:
McGraw-Hill Education
8787 Orion Place
Columbus, OH 43240

2

What ran fast?
A rat did pass Pat's class.

7

Pat's class was on a trip.

3

What can hop past?

6

123

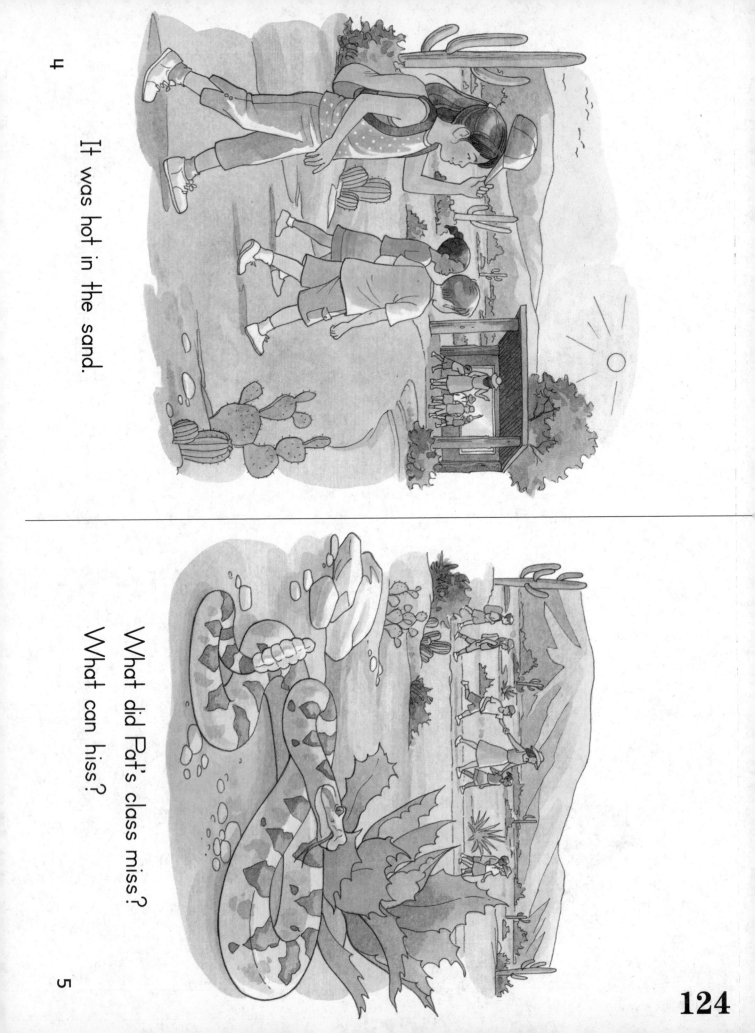

It was hot in the sand.

4

What did Pat's class miss?
What can hiss?

5

124

Rag Bits

by Greg Frazier

illustrated by Olivia Cole

Core Decodable 26

Mc Graw Hill Education

Bothell, WA • Chicago, IL • Columbus, OH • New York, NY

Mom got a pig gift.

It was a pig flag.

MHEonline.com

Mom was a pig fan.
Nan had a rag gift.

Mom had a big bag.

3

Nan had a plan.
Nan got the bag.

6

127

The bag had a tag.

"Grab the bag and look," said Mom.

A Jog in Fog

by Jesse Griffin

illustrated by C. A. Nobens

Core Decodable 27

Mc Graw Hill Education

Bothell, WA • Chicago, IL • Columbus, OH • New York, NY

Jill can jog!

Jill can see in the fog!

129

Jill is at the rocks.

Can Jill jog?

7

130

Jack is a dog on a hilltop.

3

Jan cannot jog in fog.

6

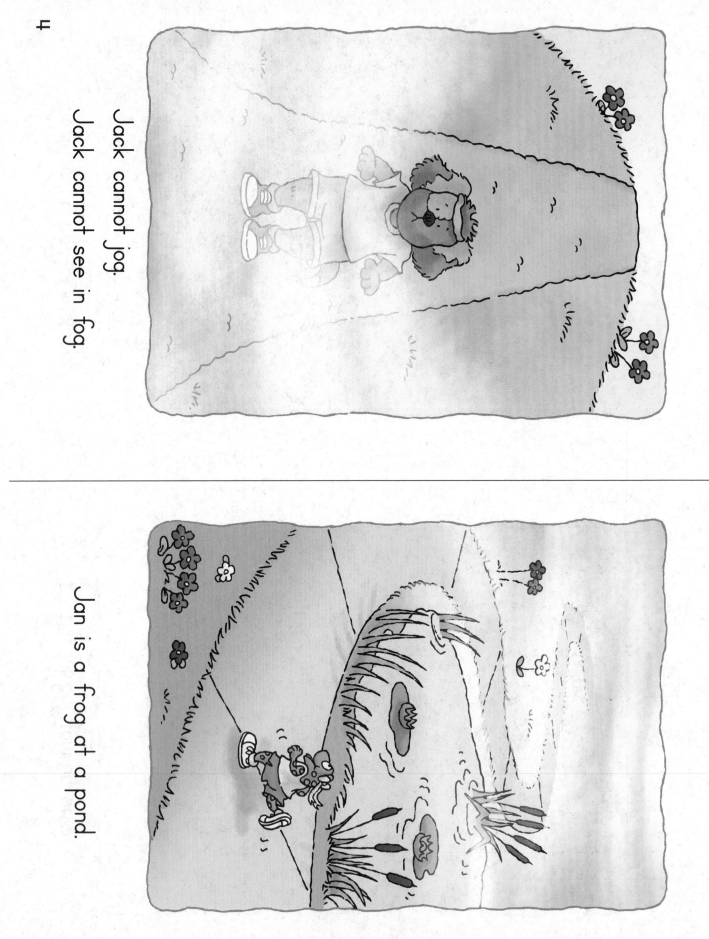

4

Jack cannot jog.
Jack cannot see in fog.

Jan is a frog at a pond.

5

A Cap Fan

by Gavin Hoffman
illustrated by Merrill Rainey

Core Decodable 28

Mc Graw Hill Education

Bothell, WA • Chicago, IL • Columbus, OH • New York, NY

Ross is a big cap fan!

16

133

Got caps? Call Ross!
Ross can pick the caps up.

Ross has on a Bobcat cap.

If a cap rips, Ross still has it.

135

Is Ross a Bobcat fan?

Ross can jam on the tan cap.

Ross is not a big Bobcat fan.

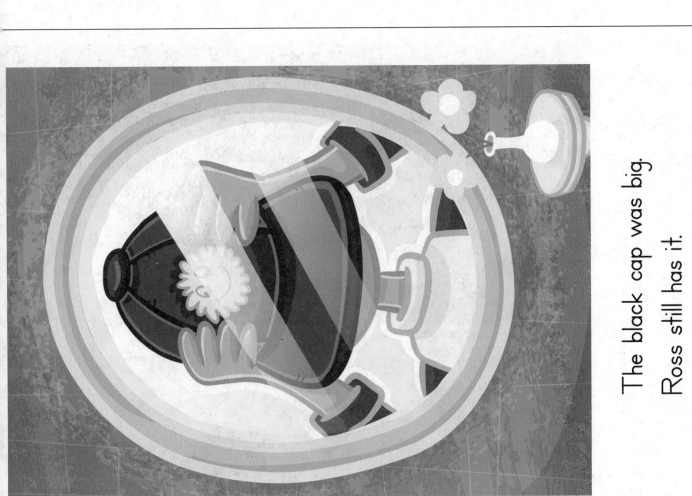

The black cap was big.

Ross still has it.

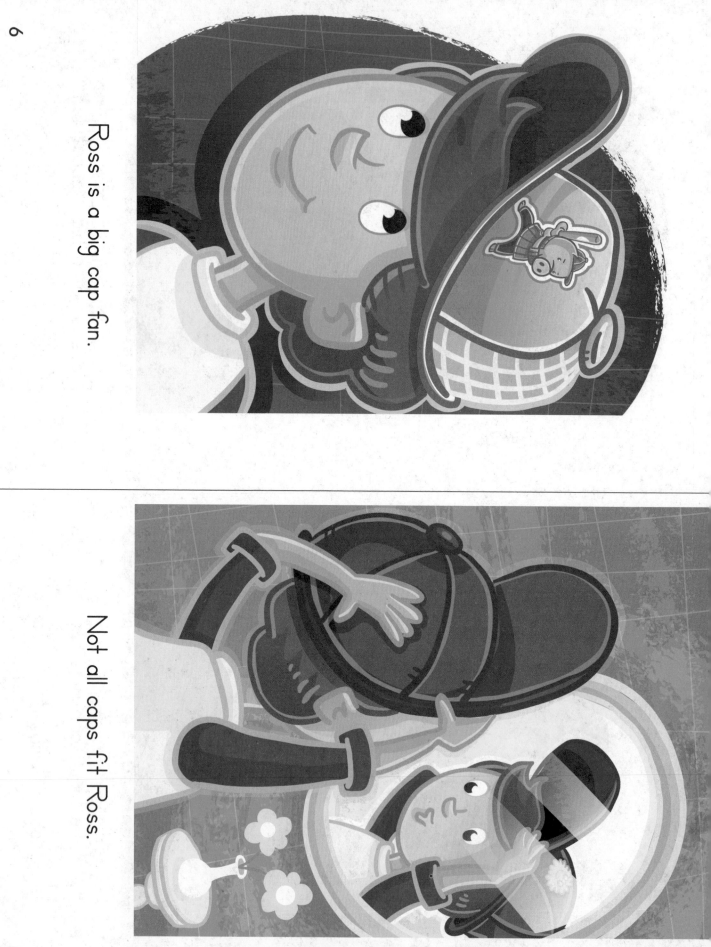

Ross is a big cap fan.

Not all caps fit Ross.

Ross has Pig, Ants, and Frog caps.

7

Ross sticks soft caps in bags.

10

139

Ross has camp and band caps.

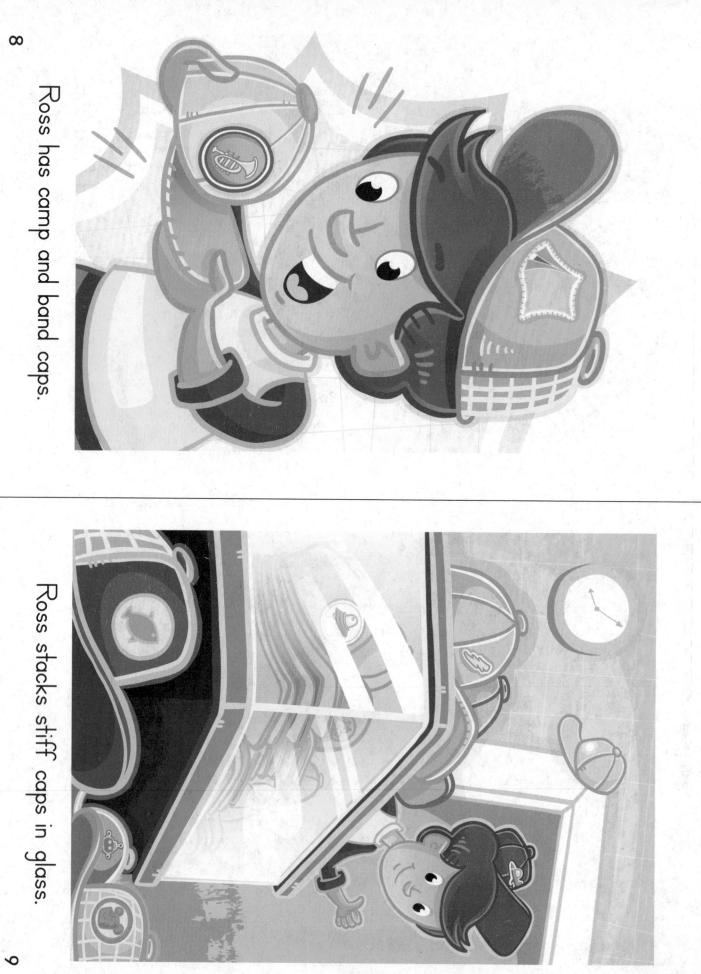

Ross stacks stiff caps in glass.

Jack's Job

by Robert Bridges
illustrated by Meryl Henderson

Core Decodable 29

Mc Graw Hill Education

Bothell, WA • Chicago, IL • Columbus, OH • New York, NY

Jack got the bridge traffic to pass.

8

141

2

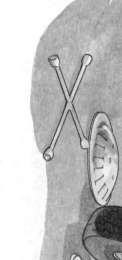

Bridge traffic had to pass.

7

142

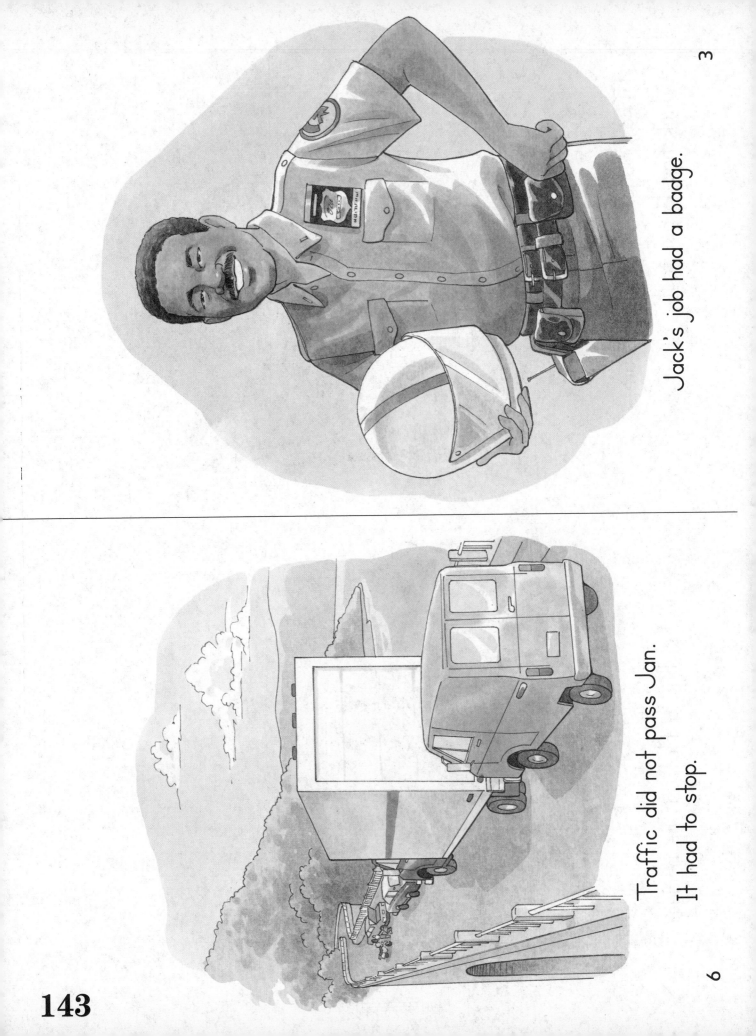

Jack's job had a badge.

Traffic did not pass Jan.
It had to stop.

3

6

143

4

The bridge had a traffic jam.
Jack had to act fast.

Jan had a flat on the bridge.

5

144

Plum Pond

by Bud Hamilton

illustrated by Deborah Colvin Borgo

Core Decodable 30

Mc Graw Hill Education

Bothell, WA • Chicago, IL • Columbus, OH • New York, NY

Plum Pond is fun!

8

A big bug sat in mud.
"Did it get stuck?" said Jill.

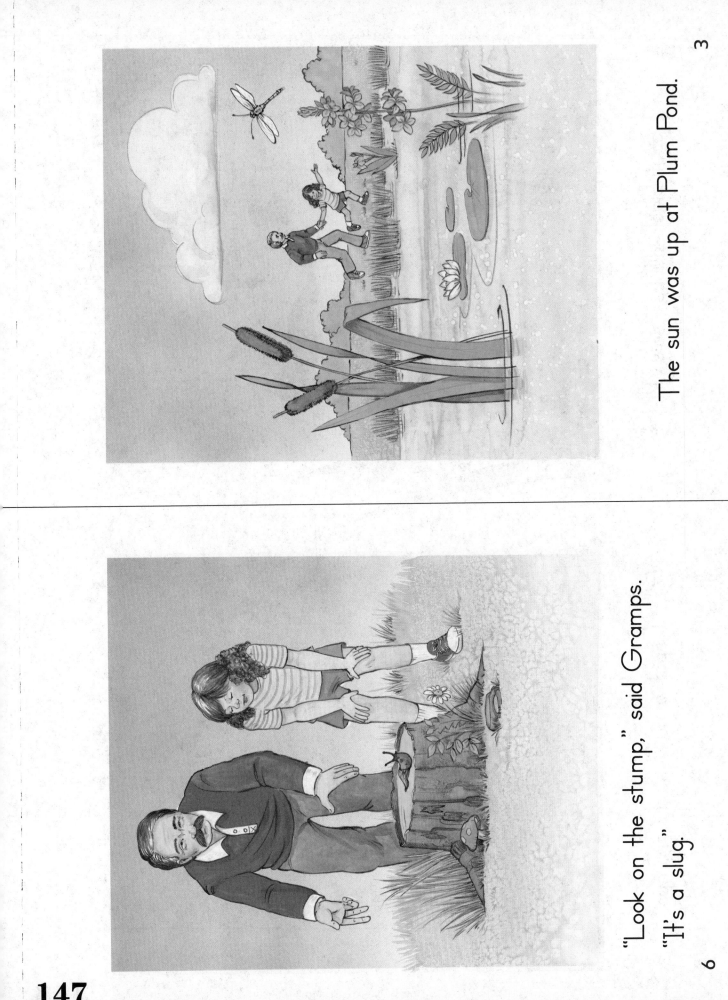

The sun was up at Plum Pond.

3

"Look on the stump," said Gramps.
"It's a slug."

6

147

"I spot black ducks," said Jill.

"Plus I spot a gull," said Gramps.

Buzz and Zip

by Tamera Williams

illustrated by Kersti Frigell

Core Decodable 31

Mc Graw Hill Education

Bothell, WA • Chicago, IL • Columbus, OH • New York, NY

Zack the bug can!

8

149

Send all inquiries to:
McGraw-Hill Education
8787 Orion Place
Columbus, OH 43240

2

"What can buzz and zip?" asks Liz.

7

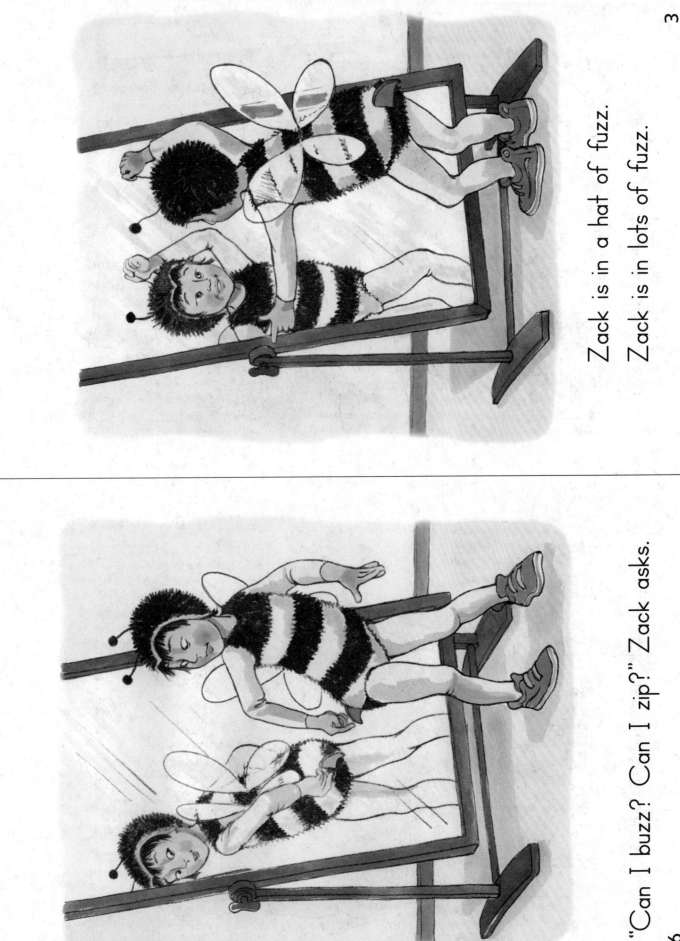

Zack is in a hat of fuzz.

Zack is in lots of fuzz.

3

"Can I buzz? Can I zip?" Zack asks.

6

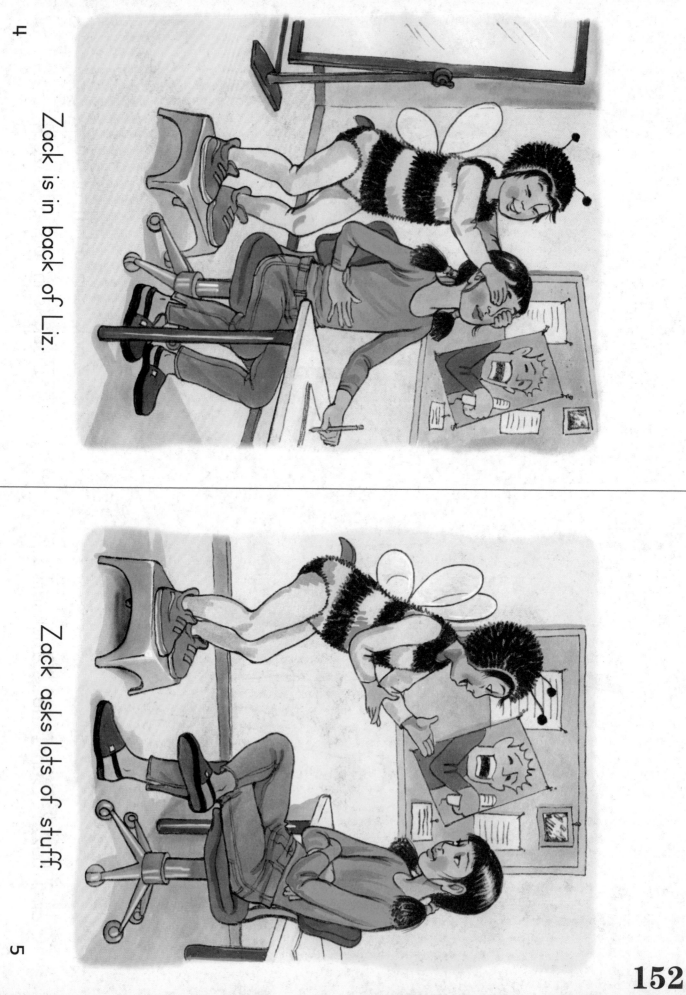

Zack is in back of Liz.

Zack asks lots of stuff.

Hills of Fuzz

by Tamera Williams
illustrated by Kersti Frigell

Core Decodable 32

Mc Graw Hill Education

Bothell, WA • Chicago, IL • Columbus, OH • New York, NY

153

"Is he still a bug?" asks Liz.

"I am Zack," he grins.

8

Zack stops.
He stands in hills of fuzz.

154

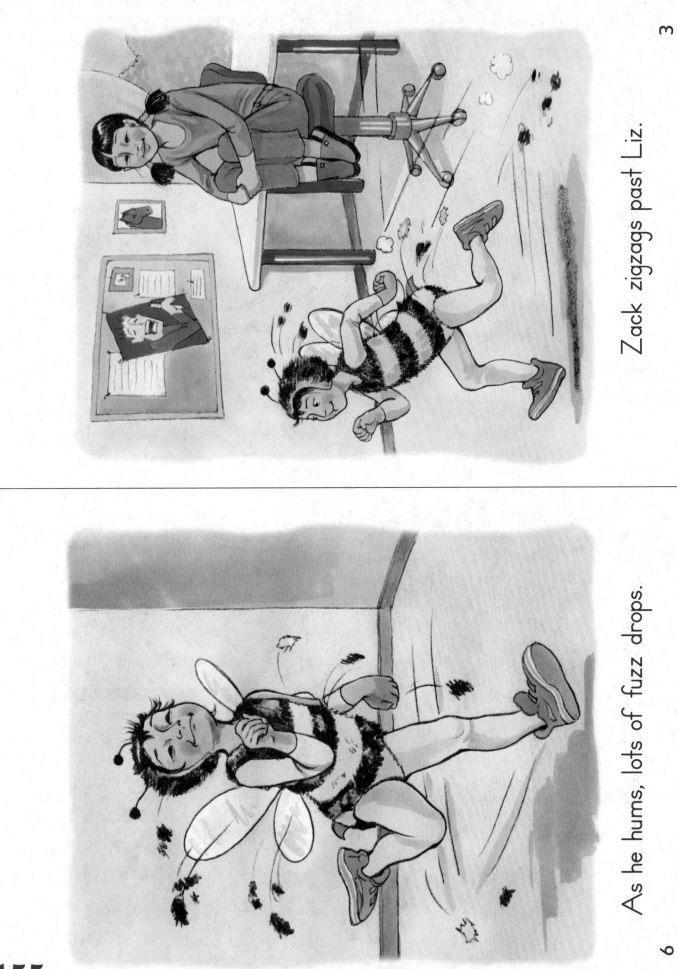

Zack zigzags past Liz.

As he hums, lots of fuzz drops.

3

6

As he zags, bits of fuzz drop.

4

Zack hums as he zigs and zags.

5

Rock and Jazz

by Bud Hamilton
illustrated by Lynne Avril

Core Decodable 33

Mc Graw Hill Education

Bothell, WA • Chicago, IL • Columbus, OH • New York, NY

Dad has his plugs.

16

Mom has on muffs.

In the attic, Jim has drums.

Jim hits his drums.

3

Mom has a gift of plugs.

14

159

Jim's drumsticks hit and hit.

Bam! Bam! Bam!

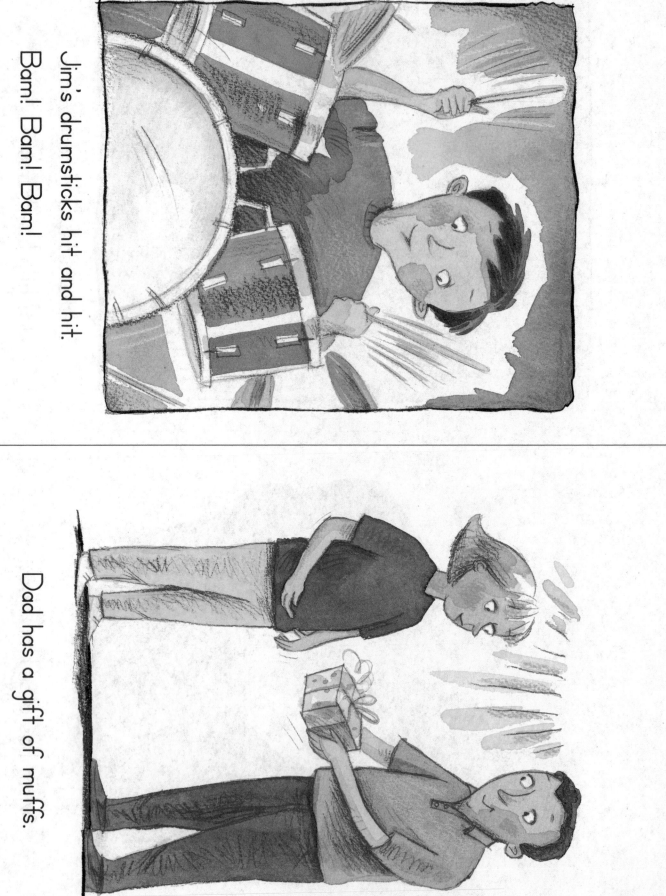

Dad has a gift of muffs.

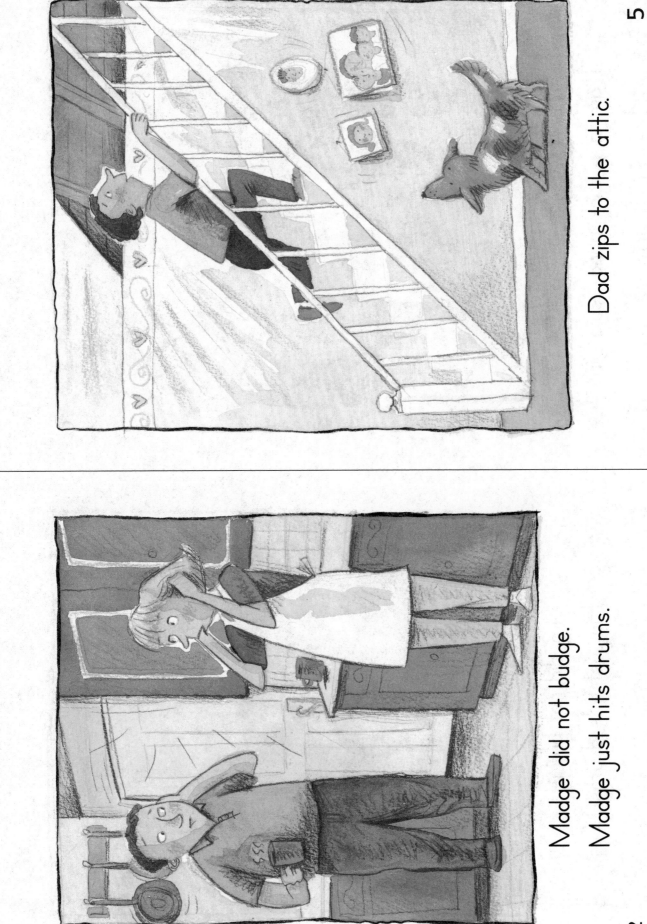

Madge did not budge.
Madge just hits drums.

12

Dad zips to the attic.

5

"I am in a rock band," said Jim.

Jim did not budge.
He just hits drums.

11

In back, Madge has drums.
Madge hits the drums.

7

"I am in a jazz band," said Madge.

10

163

Bam! Bam! Bam!
Madge's drumsticks hit and hit.

8

Mom zips to the back.

9

Max and Sam

by Rebecca Blankenhorn
illustrated by Barry Mullins

Core Decodable 34

Mc Graw Hill Education

Bothell, WA • Chicago, IL • Columbus, OH • New York, NY

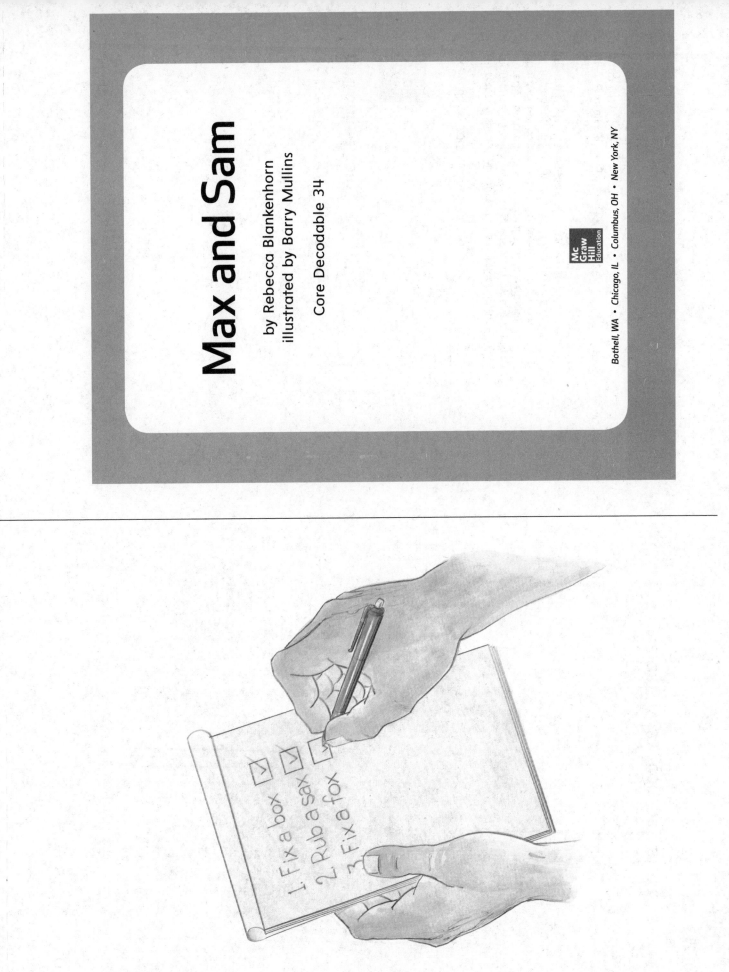

1. Fix a box
2. Rub a sax
3. Fix a fox

MHEonline.com

![Mc Graw Hill Education]

Send all inquiries to:
McGraw-Hill Education
8787 Orion Place
Columbus, OH 43240

2

Last, Max can list stuff.

7

166

167

Max and Sam fix stuff.

Max and Sam fix a fox.

4

Max and Sam fix a box.

Max can rub a sax.
Can Sam rub a sax?

5

A Red Fox

by Joaquin Garcia
illustrated by Pat Lucas-Morris

Core Decodable 35

Mc Graw Hill Education

Bothell, WA • Chicago, IL • Columbus, OH • New York, NY

At sun-up, a red fox rests. It sits down.

8

2

A red fox can smell hens.

7

170

A red fox has a den.

A red fox can hunt down a rabbit.

4

Its den is down in grass.

If the sun is down, a red fox hunts.

5

The Glass

by Antonio Colantoni
illustrated by Mark Corcoran

Core Decodable 36

Mc Graw Hill Education

Bothell, WA • Chicago, IL • Columbus, OH • New York, NY

173

Mom sat up and lifted the glass.
"I cannot sip!" said Mom.

8

Bugs buzzed back to the nest.

Mom filled a glass.

3

Bugs buzzed in a glass.

6

175

As Mom rested, a bug smelled the glass.
What was in it?

4

The bug visited its nest.

5

176

Best Mom

by Lisa Boggs

illustrated by Kersti Frigell

Core Decodable 37

Mc Graw Hill Education

Bothell, WA • Chicago, IL • Columbus, OH • New York, NY

Dad handed Tom a pin.

Tom pinned it on Mom.

The pin said BEST MOM.

8

Dad landed.
Mom picked him up.

Tom slipped.
Mom helped him up.

3

Tom acted.
Mom clapped.

6

179

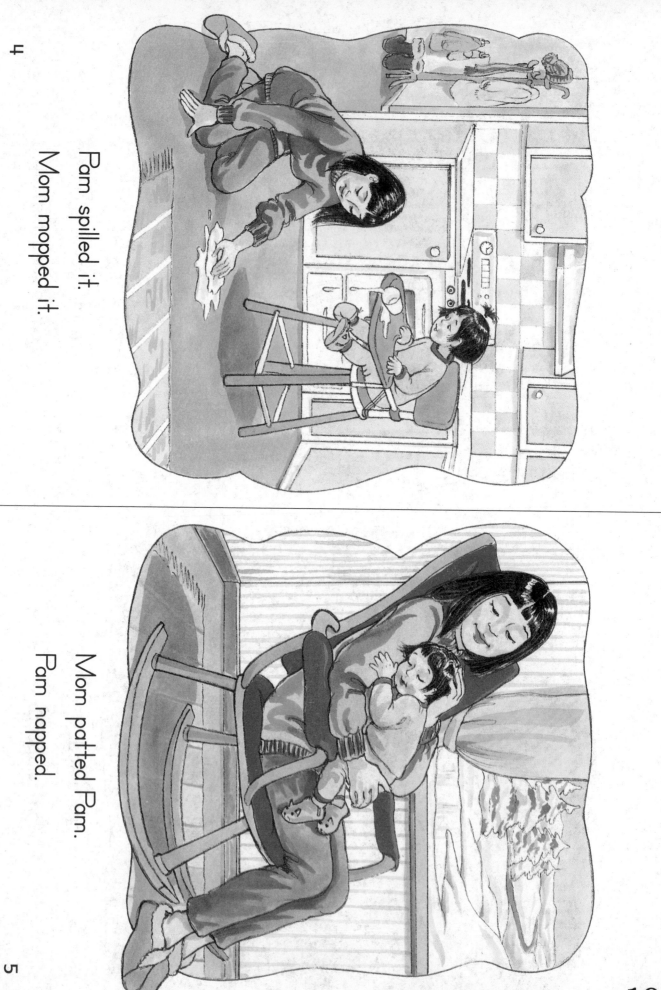

Pam spilled it.
Mom mopped it.

Mom patted Pam.
Pam napped.

4

5

180

Fix a Truck

by Jessica Evans

illustrated by Meryl Henderson

Core Decodable 38

Bothell, WA • Chicago, IL • Columbus, OH • New York, NY

The men set stuff back in the truck.

16

181

2

The men fixed the truck.

15

183

A red truck had a flat.
It was stuck.

3

The truck budged!

14

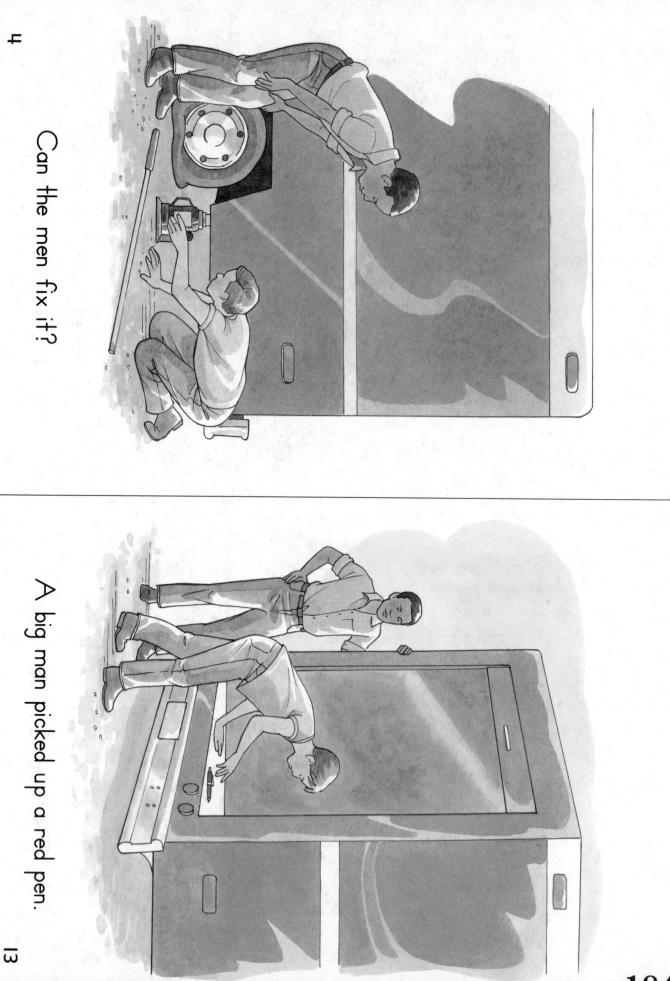

Can the men fix it?

4

A big man picked up a red pen.

13

184

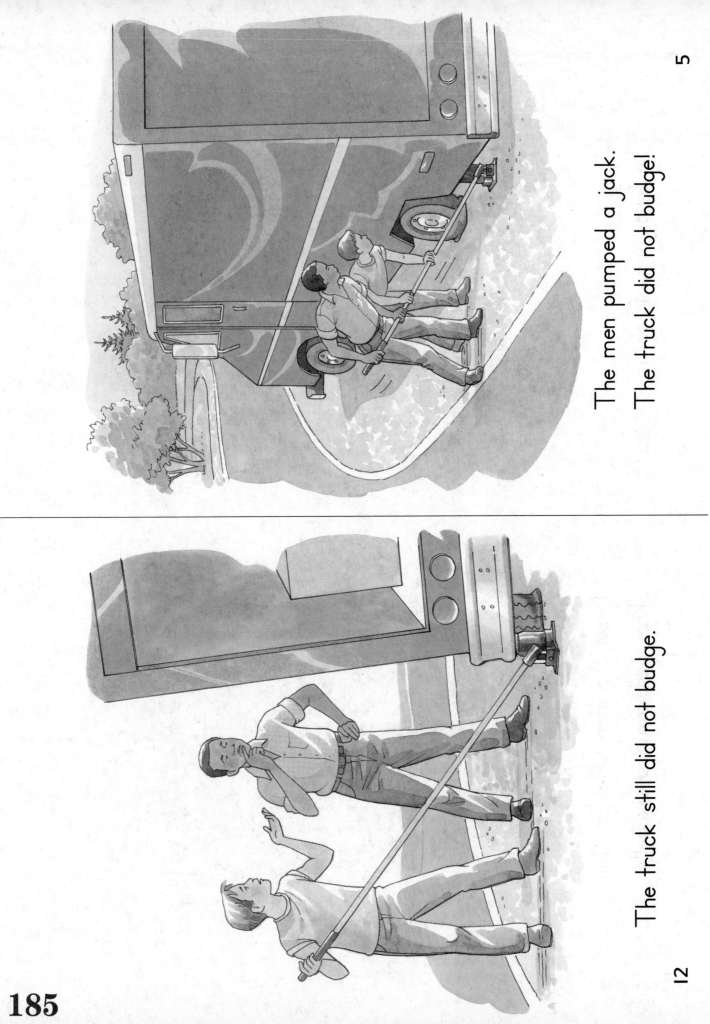

The men pumped a jack.
The truck did not budge!

5

The truck still did not budge.

12

185

The truck was filled up.

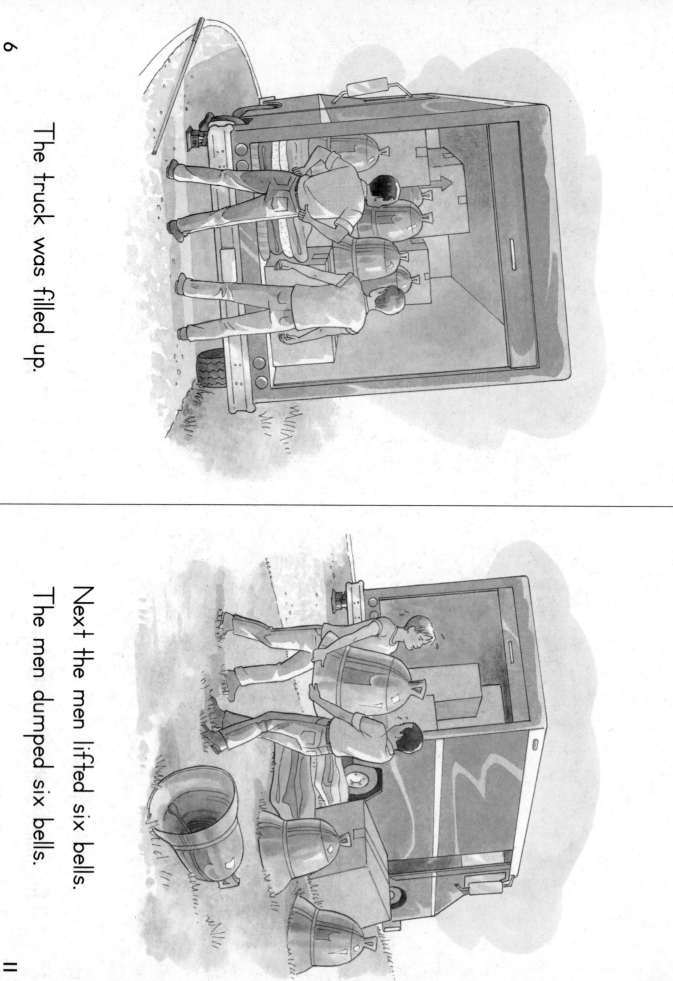

Next the men lifted six bells.
The men dumped six bells.

The men lifted a big box.
The men set it down.

The truck did not budge!

7

187

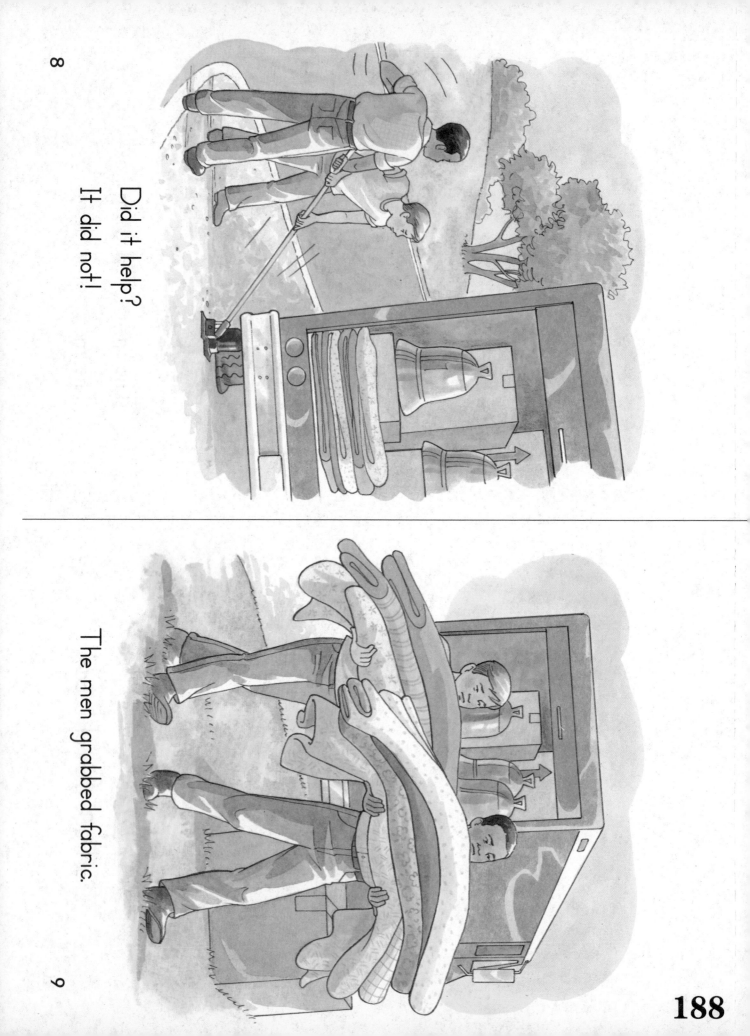

Did it help?
It did not!

The men grabbed fabric.

Ted's List

by Antonio Colantoni

illustrated by Mary Maass

Core Decodable 39

Mc Graw Hill Education

Bothell, WA • Chicago, IL • Columbus, OH • New York, NY

"I dreamt of jam and bread!"

MHEonline.com

Send all inquiries to:
McGraw-Hill Education
8787 Orion Place
Columbus, OH 43240

Dad fixed eggs.

Then, Ted spread jam on bread.

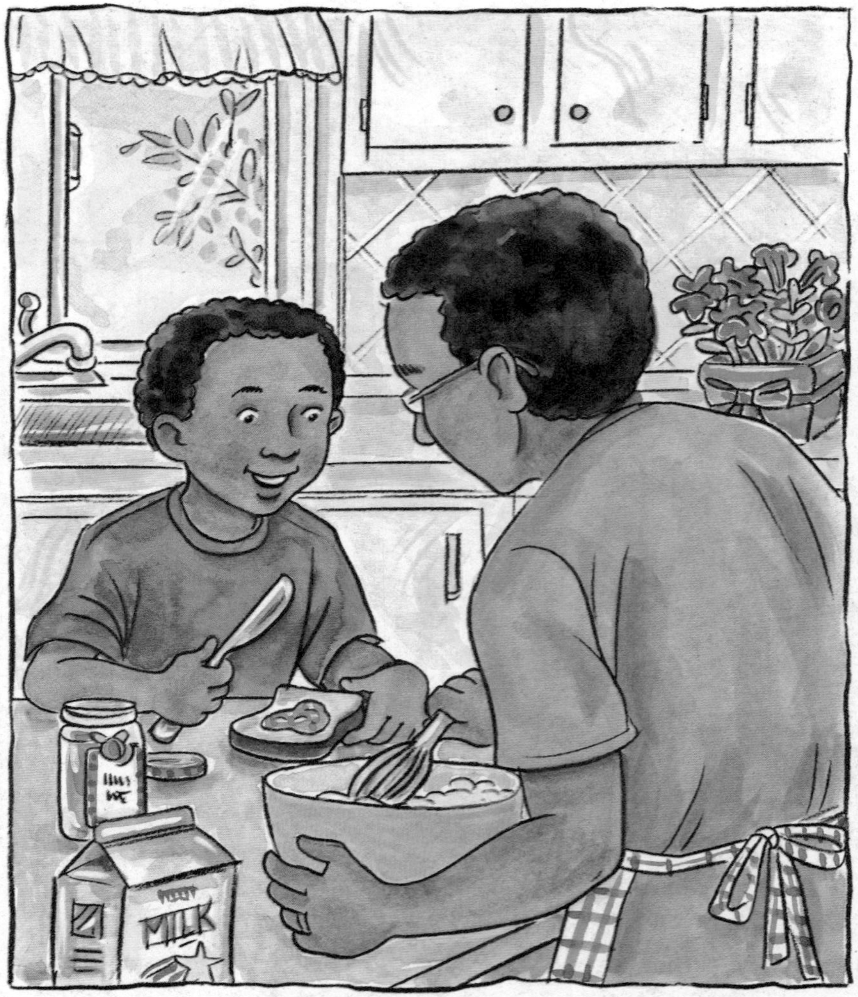

Ted printed his list.

3

Dad and Ted then headed back.

6

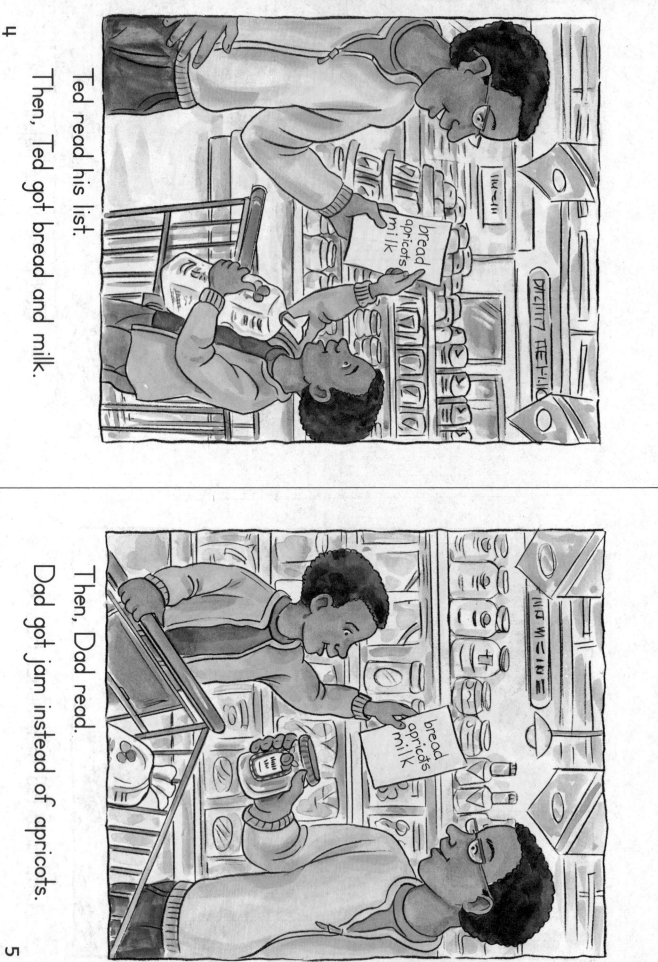

4

Ted read his list.

Then, Ted got bread and milk.

Then, Dad read.

Dad got jam instead of apricots.

5

Trish's Ship

by Ron Hart

illustrated by Jan Pyk

Core Decodable 40

Mc Graw Hill Education

Bothell, WA • Chicago, IL • Columbus, OH • New York, NY

Trish's ship splashes in the sun.

2

Trish calls the ship "The Shellfish."

7

194

195

Trish fishes.
Trish picks up shells.

3

Trish has a plan. Trish gets Mom.
Trish brushes the sand.

6

Can Trish spot a ship?
Is it stashed in the shed?

4

It is! A ship is stashed in the shed.

5

Beth Gets a Snack

by Trisha Roberts

illustrated by Shawn McManus

Core Decodable 41

Mc Graw Hill Education

Bothell, WA • Chicago, IL • Columbus, OH • New York, NY

Beth is not thin.

Thick thread is in Beth!

197

8

2

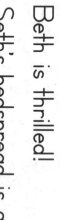

Beth is thrilled!
Seth's bedspread is a snack.

7

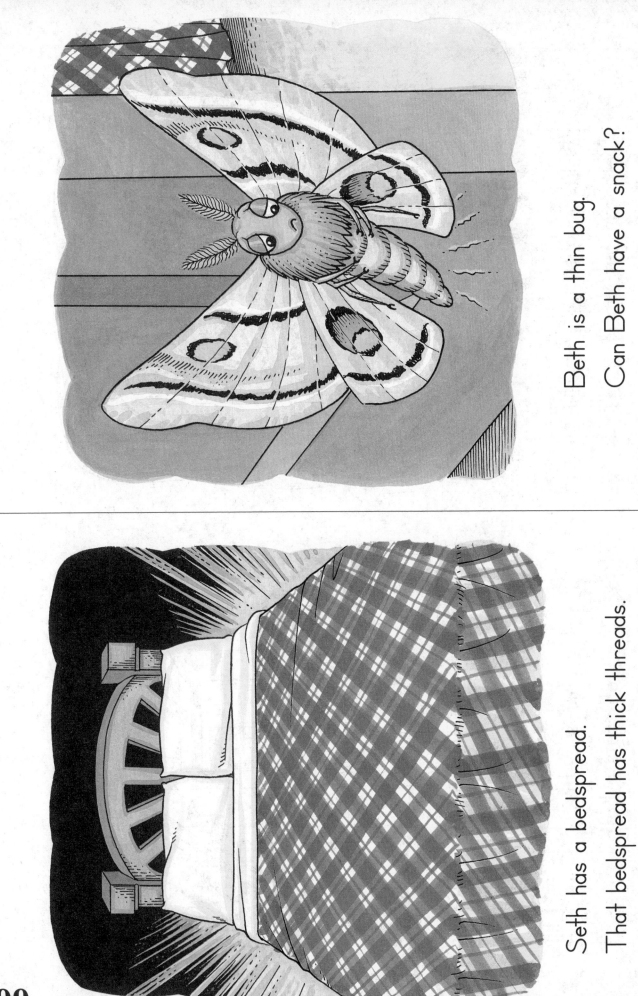

Beth is a thin bug.
Can Beth have a snack?

Seth has a bedspread.
That bedspread has thick threads.

Is fabric a snack?

Beth can get fabric.

4

This is Seth.

Seth gets a bath.

5

200

Mitch on a Ranch

by Rhonda Martin

illustrated by Meryl Henderson

Core Decodable 42

Bothell, WA • Chicago, IL • Columbus, OH • New York, NY

Mc Graw Hill Education

201

Dad pats Patch.

Mitch gets Patch a snack.

8

Patch catches on and helps.
The truck is not in the ditch.

202

This is Mitch.
Mitch is on a ranch.

Dad's truck is stuck in a ditch!
Mitch fetches Patch.

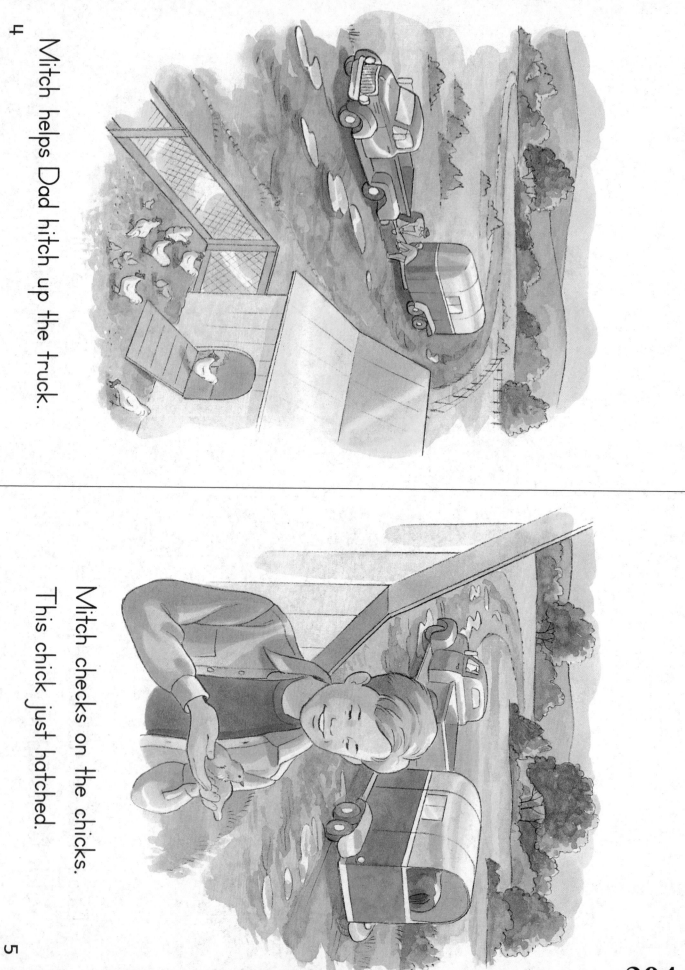

4

Mitch helps Dad hitch up the truck.

Mitch checks on the chicks.
This chick just hatched.

5

Ball Camp

by Antonio Colantoni
illustrated by Meryl Henderson

Core Decodable 43

Mc Graw Hill Education

Bothell, WA • Chicago, IL • Columbus, OH • New York, NY

"It was fun on the bench," said Mitch.

"And it is fun to hit, pitch, and catch!"

16

Mitch jumps to catch the ball!

Beth, Trish, and Chad jump and clap.

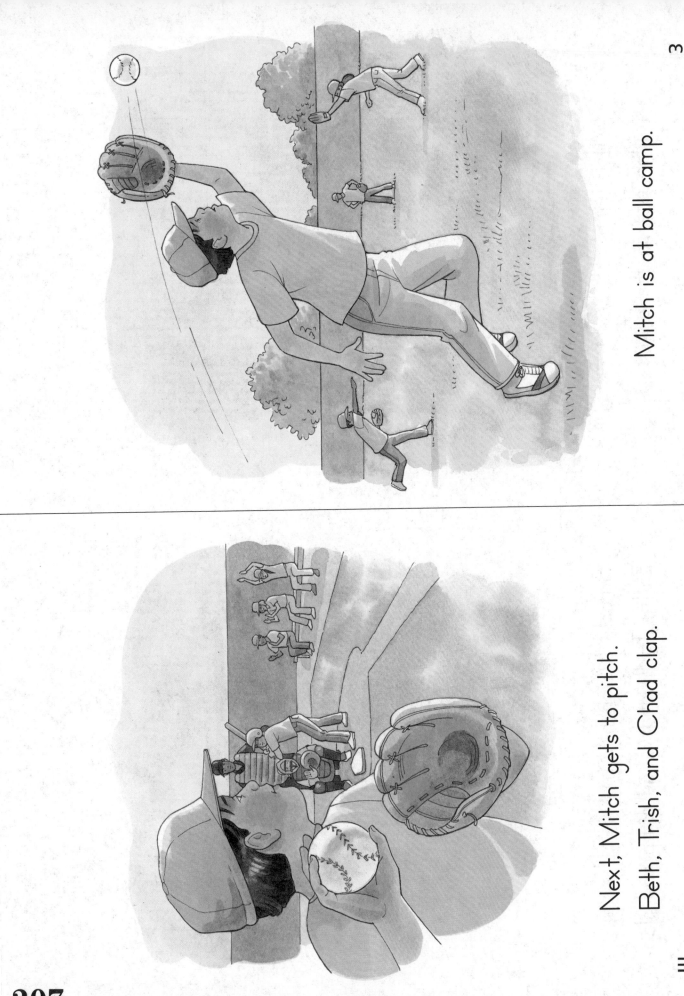

Mitch is at ball camp.

Next, Mitch gets to pitch.
Beth, Trish, and Chad clap.

3

14

Mitch is not the best.
Mitch sits on the bench.

Smash! Mitch hits it!
Beth, Trish, and Chad jump and clap.

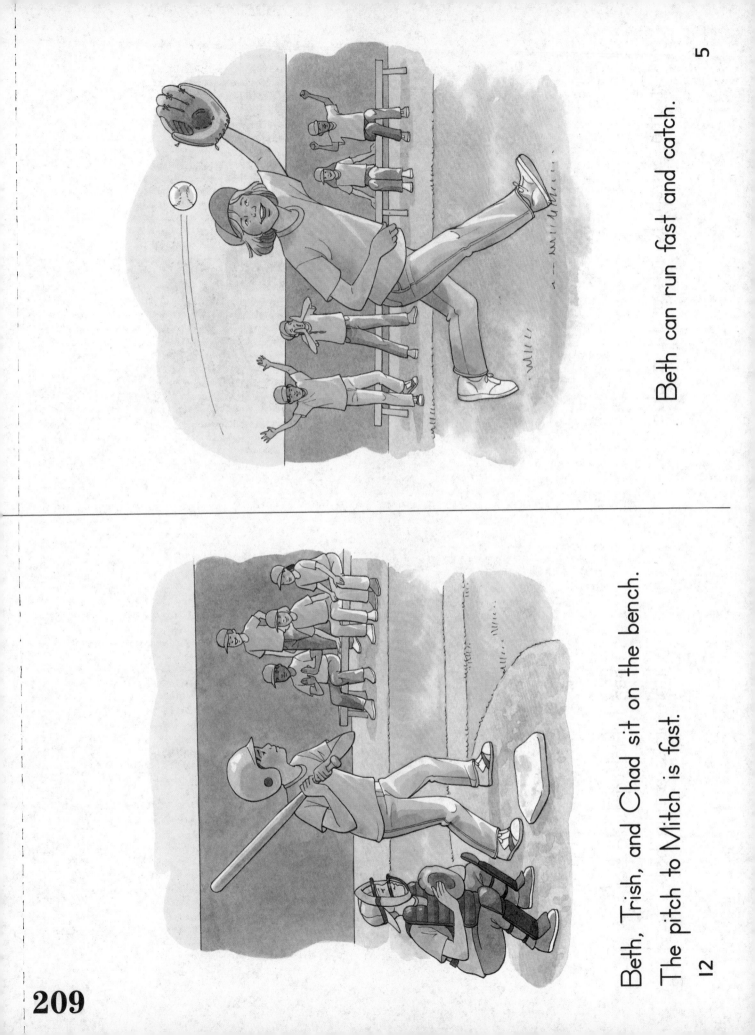

Beth can run fast and catch.

5

Beth, Trish, and Chad sit on the bench.

The pitch to Mitch is fast.

12

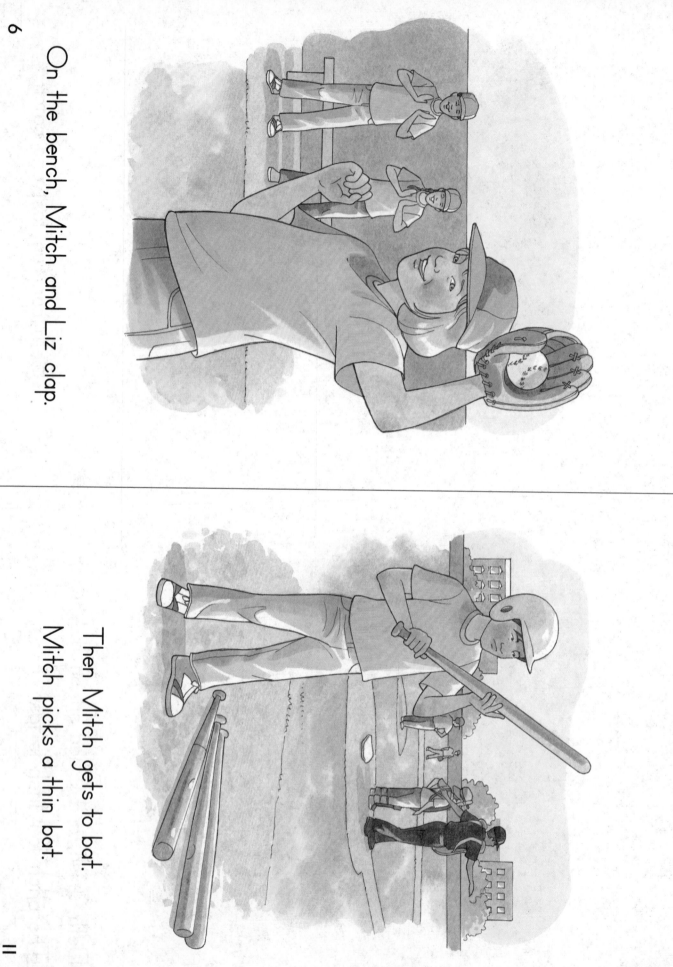

On the bench, Mitch and Liz clap.

6

Then Mitch gets to bat.
Mitch picks a thin bat.

11

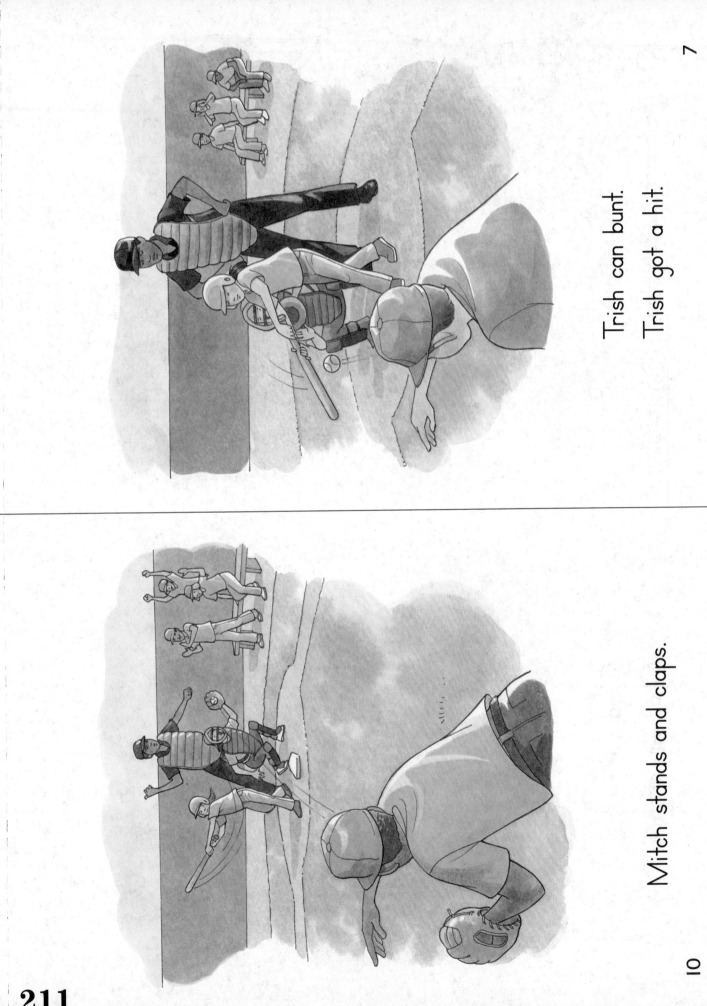

Trish can bunt.
Trish got a hit.

Mitch stands and claps.

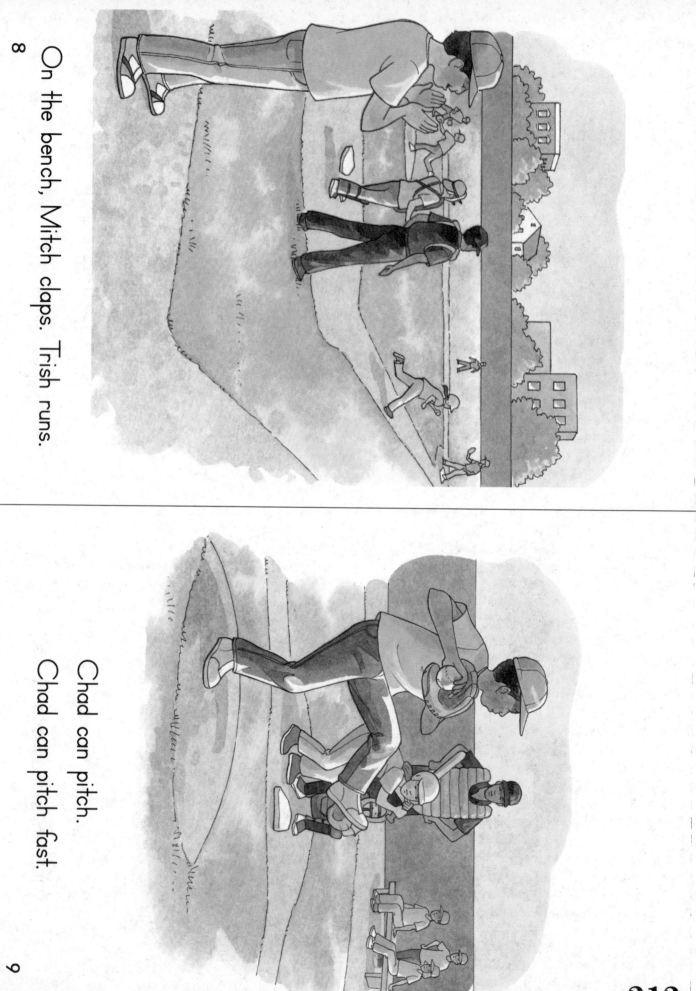

On the bench, Mitch claps. Trish runs.

8

Chad can pitch.
Chad can pitch fast.

9

At a Port

by Alex Yu
illustrated by Meryl Henderson

Core Decodable 44

Mc Graw Hill Education

Bothell, WA • Chicago, IL • Columbus, OH • New York, NY

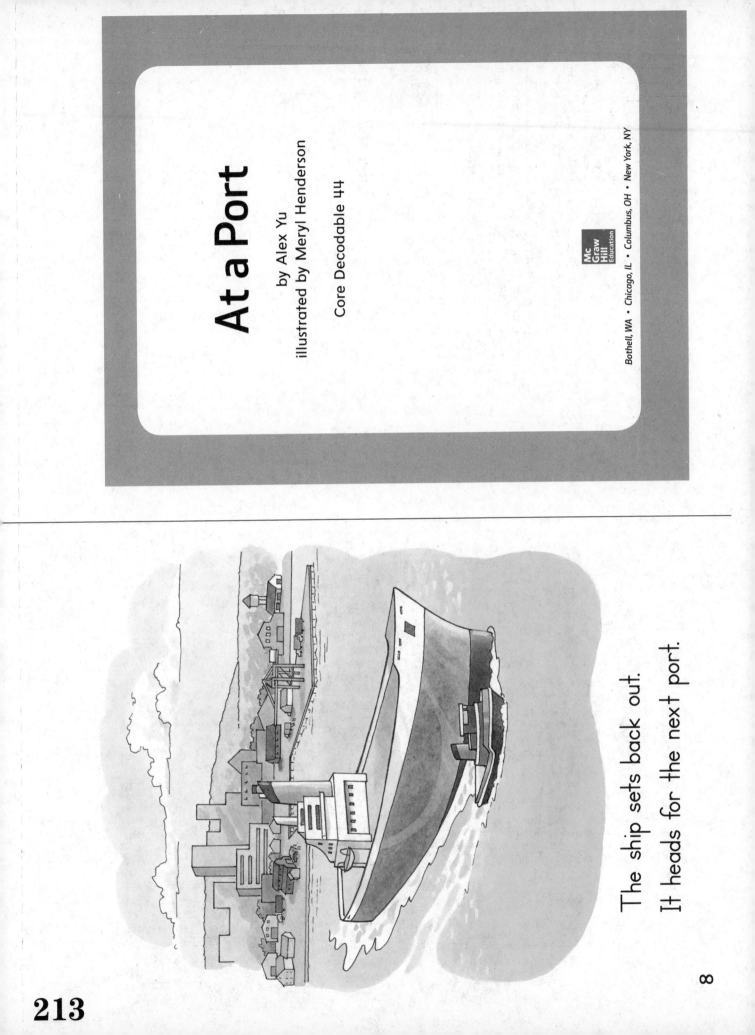

The ship sets back out.

It heads for the next port.

8

2

This is a forklift.

It gets more out of the ship.

7

214

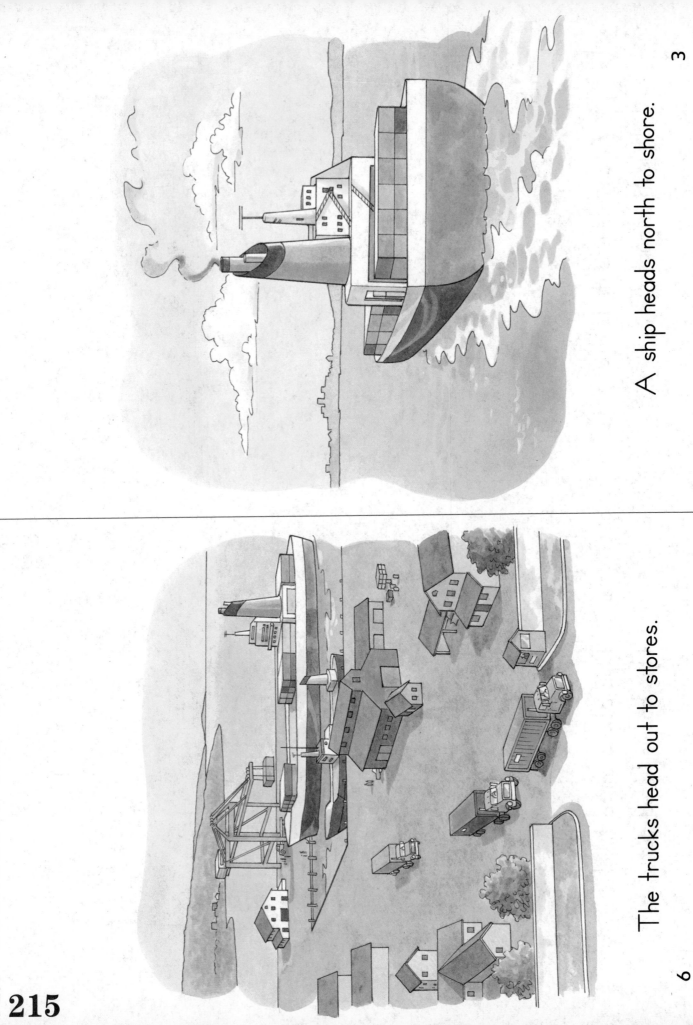

A ship heads north to shore.

3

The trucks head out to stores.

6

215

A ship blasts its horn.

It is in a port.

This box is for a truck.

This box is lifted out.

4

5

In a Jar

by Charles Broderick
illustrated by Mary Maass

Core Decodable 45

Mc Graw Hill Education

Bothell, WA • Chicago, IL • Columbus, OH • New York, NY

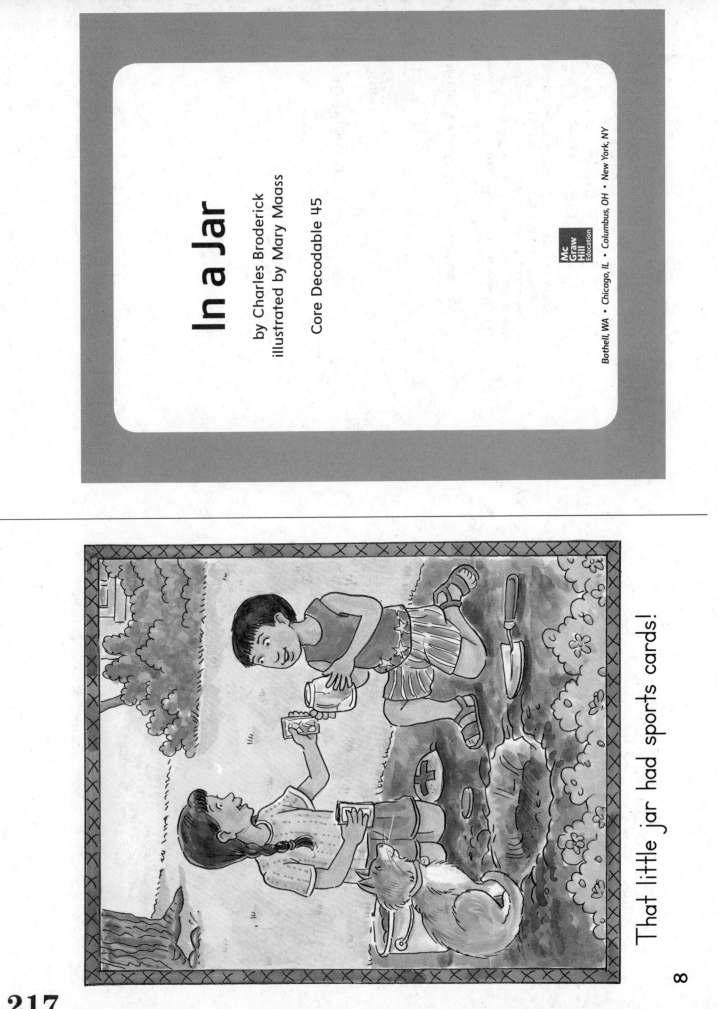

That little jar had sports cards!

8

2

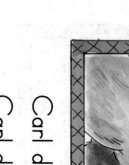

Carl dug a little more.
Carl dug until he hit a jar.

7

Gramps sent a little card to Carl and Barb.

3

Carl started to dig in dark mud.

6

Carl and Barb read the card:
Dig at a red mark in the garden.

Hugs,
Gramps

Barb spotted a little red mark.

The twig went. Wes is wet, and Gwen is wet!

8

Wes Gets Wet

by Emma Green

illustrated by Len Epstein

Core Decodable 46

Mc Graw Hill Education

Bothell, WA • Chicago, IL • Columbus, OH • New York, NY

MHEonline.com

Send all inquiries to:
McGraw-Hill Education
8787 Orion Place
Columbus, OH 43240

The wind grabs a twig. Wes jumps and runs. Wes is swift!

Gwen scrubs Dad's truck.

Wes trots to help.

3

Wes sits and sits.

6

Gwen tells Wes to sit next to the wall.
Will Wes get wet there?

4

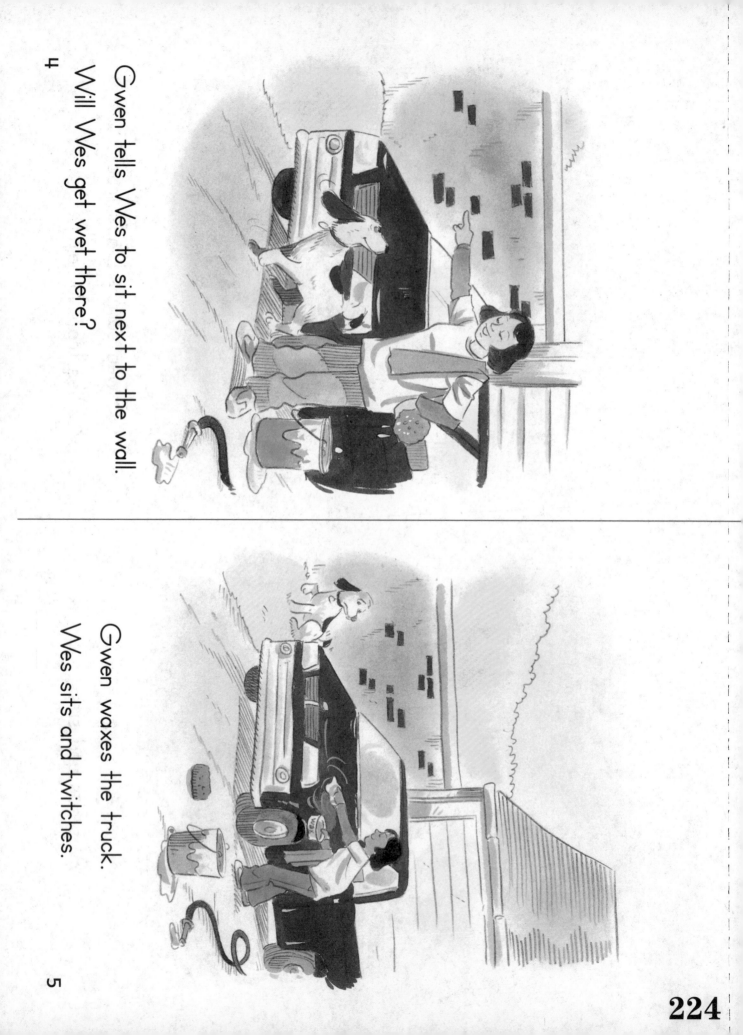

Gwen waxes the truck.
Wes sits and twitches.

5

The Whiz

by Mark Decker
illustrated by Len Epstein

Core Decodable 47

Mc Graw Hill Education

Bothell, WA • Chicago, IL • Columbus, OH • New York, NY

Wham! When the Whiz stops, it stops fast.

8

2

The Whiz whips up a big hill.
Then it whips past a bridge.

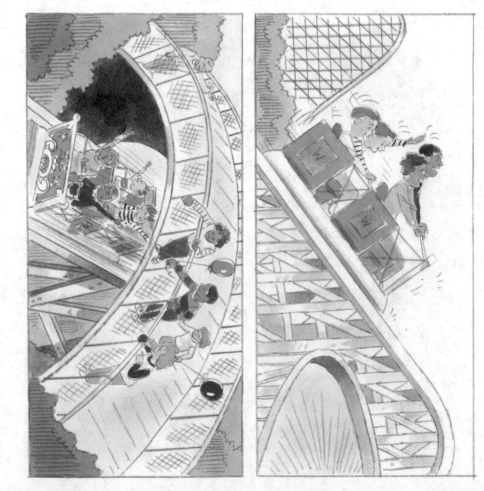

227

This is the Whiz.

3

Wham! The Whiz whips left.
Wham! The Whiz whips back.

6

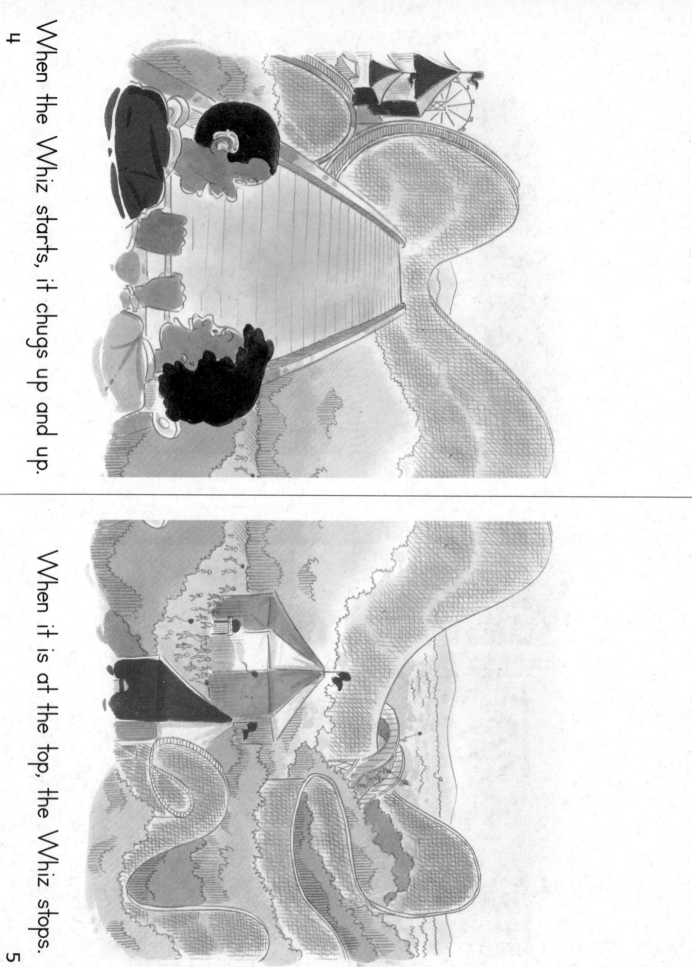

When the Whiz starts, it chugs up and up.

4

When it is at the top, the Whiz stops.

5

A Spark in the Dark

by Thomas Sato
illustrated by Benton Mahan

Core Decodable 48

Mc Graw Hill Education

Bothell, WA • Chicago, IL • Columbus, OH • New York, NY

"A spark in the dark," said Carmen.

8

2

"That is a bug," said Corbin.
"I will catch more in a jar."

7

Mom sits on the porch.
The twins whiz past.

"What a star!" said Carmen.
"I wish I had that star."

4

When it is dark, the stars are out.

Carmen spots a little star.
It is not far up.

5

Bird Shirts

by Trisha Roberts
illustrated by Kersti Frigell

Core Decodable 49

Mc
Graw
Hill
Education

Bothell, WA • Chicago, IL • Columbus, OH • New York, NY

As a matter of fact, there was!

8

2

Amber's last gift was a shirt.
Was there a bird on it?

7

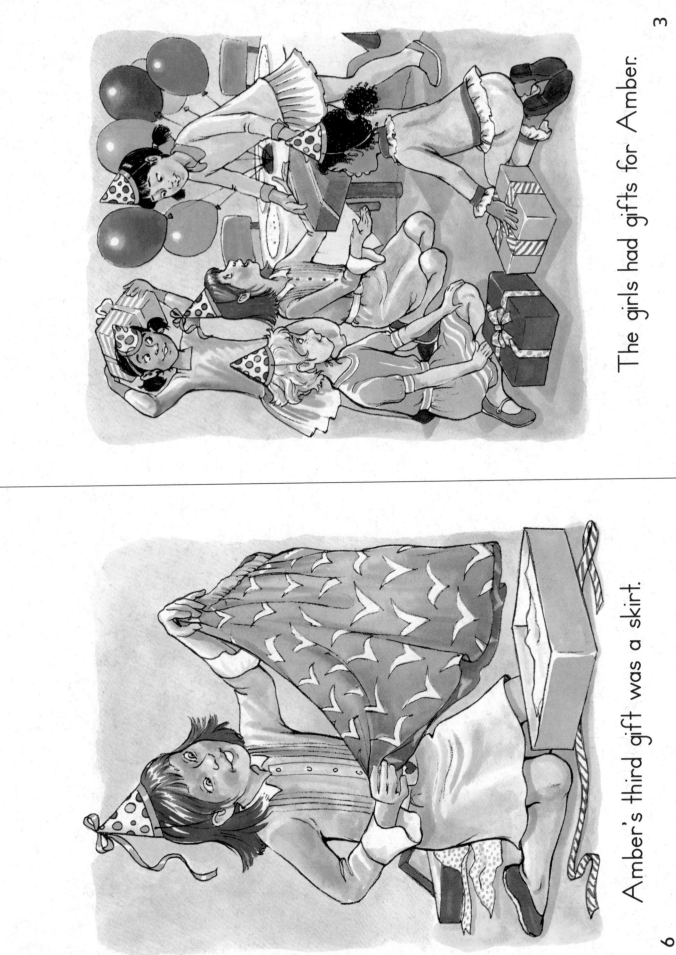

The girls had gifts for Amber.

3

Amber's third gift was a skirt.

6

4

Her first gift was a shirt.
The shirt had a bird on it.

Amber's next gift was a shirt.
It had a bigger bird on it!

5

236

A Blur with Fur

by Chris Mathews
illustrated by Mark Corcoran

Core Decodable 50

Mc Graw Hill Education

Bothell, WA • Chicago, IL • Columbus, OH • New York, NY

It is Burt!
The blur with fur is Burt.

8

2

What is that blur with fur?

7

A blur with fur crossed the carpet.

3

The blur with fur dashed and crashed.
It curled and twirled.

6

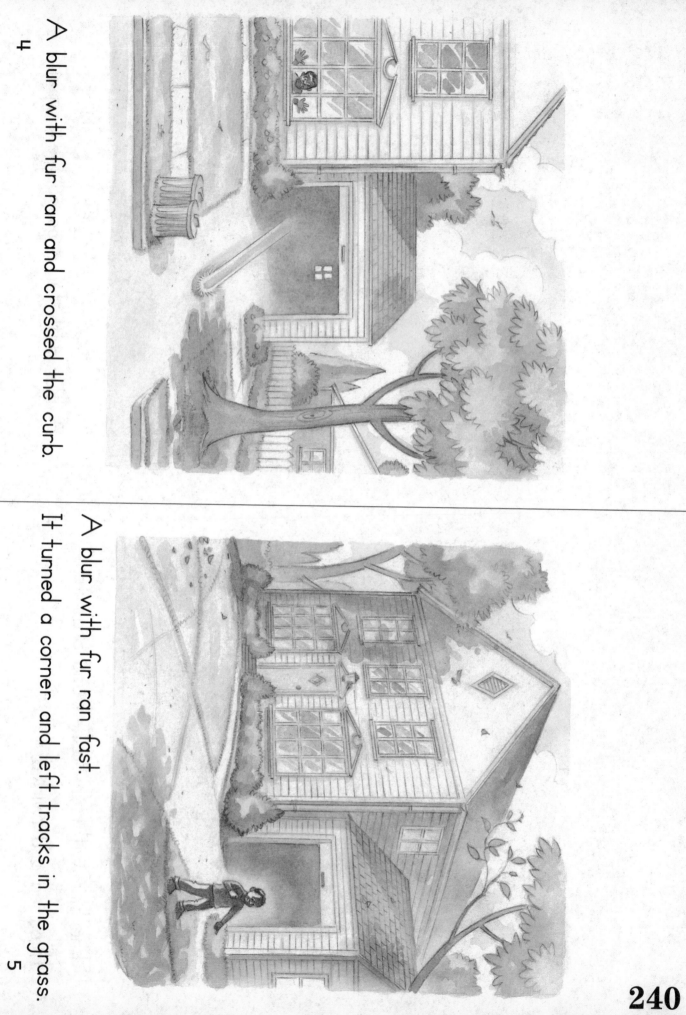

A blur with fur ran and crossed the curb.

4

A blur with fur ran fast. It turned a corner and left tracks in the grass.

5

240

Earnest's Search

by Judy Mills

illustrated by Len Ebert

Core Decodable 51

Mc Graw Hill Education

Bothell, WA • Chicago, IL • Columbus, OH • New York, NY

It is a pearl!

Earnest got a shell and a pearl!

Earnest got a shell from the water.
What is in it?

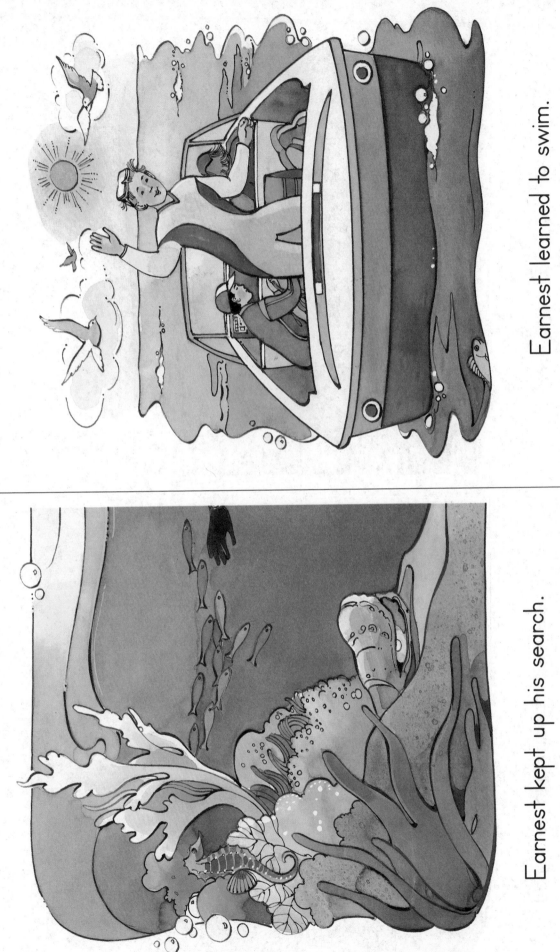

Earnest learned to swim.
Earnest liked to swim.

Earnest kept up his search.
Did Earnest get any shells?

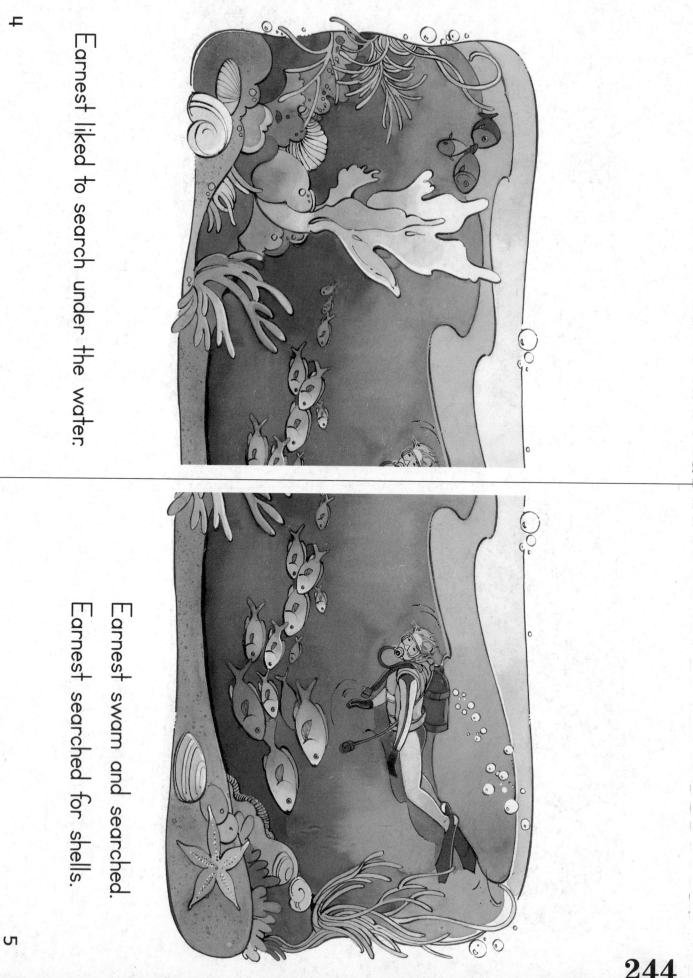

Earnest liked to search under the water.

4

Earnest swam and searched.
Earnest searched for shells.

5

244

Big Bing

by Andrea Patel
illustrated by Kersti Frigell

Core Decodable 52

Mc Graw Hill Education

Bothell, WA • Chicago, IL • Columbus, OH • New York, NY

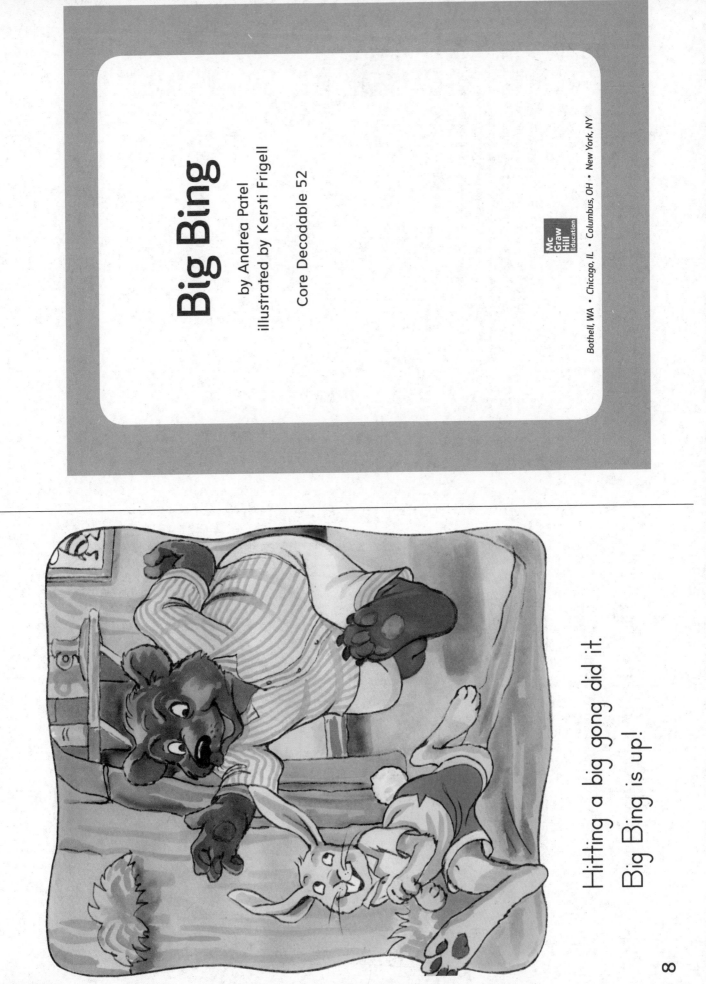

Hitting a big gong did it.
Big Bing is up!

8

245

Banging will not.
But hitting a big gong will.

246

247

It is spring.
But Big Bing is still resting.

3

Singing will not get Bing up.
Will banging do it?

6

4

Bing must get up.
Will a long ring get Bing up?

5

A long ring will not do it.
Will a song do it?

Purple

by Maria Johnson
illustrated by Susan Lexa

Core Decodable 53

Mc
Graw
Hill
Education

Bothell, WA • Chicago, IL • Columbus, OH • New York, NY

No matter where I turn,
I see a blur of purple!

8

2

Mom gets purple plants
from the earth.

7

I am a purple girl.
I have lots of purple things.

3

This pitcher has bursts of purple.
I am learning to fill cups.

6

251

I set purple shirts, skirts, and pants in my purple dresser.

I have purple strings and purple ping pong stuff.

The Children Get a Rabbit

by Rob Hip

illustrated by Barry Mullins

Core Decodable 54

Mc Graw Hill Education

Bothell, WA • Chicago, IL • Columbus, OH • New York, NY

The children and Dad get in the truck.

They had a fun trip!

2

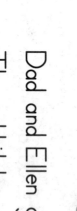

Dad and Ellen get melon.

The rabbit has a carrot.

7

Dad and the children plan a trip.
They get in a truck.

3

They pet a soft rabbit.
"Dad, can I adopt him?" asks Ellen.

6

They see an animal with a banana.

4

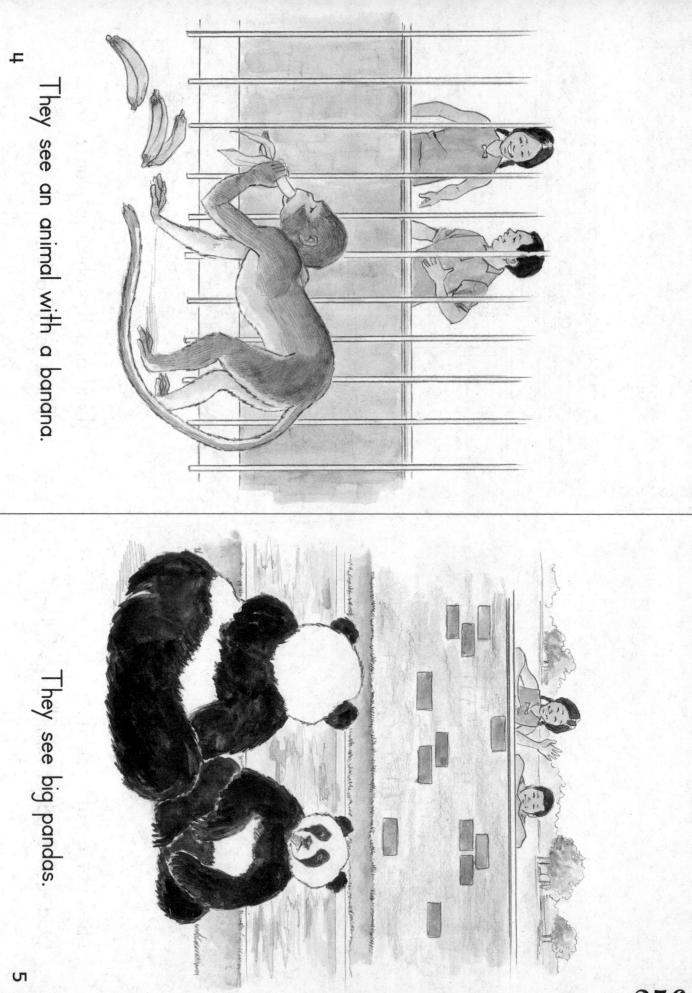

They see big pandas.

5

Pump and Pedal

by Natalie Lambert

illustrated by Meryl Henderson

Core Decodable 55

Mc Graw Hill Education

Bothell, WA • Chicago, IL • Columbus, OH • New York, NY

Pump to a fast finish.

Win a medal, Pat!

8

2

Pump in Fossil Park.
Pedal! Pedal! Pedal!

7

Pump fast at the signal, Pat.
Pedal to get ahead.

3

Pedal under the metal bridge.
Pump fast in the tunnel.

6

4

A big hill is not a problem.
Just pump and pedal.

Pump past a garden.
Pedal next to the dog kennel.

5

In the Tank

by Andrea Patel

illustrated by Kersti Frigell

Core Decodable 56

Mc Graw Hill Education

Bothell, WA • Chicago, IL • Columbus, OH • New York, NY

But he pops up fast.
I think I better run.

2

I did dunk Big Bing!

He sinks fast.

7

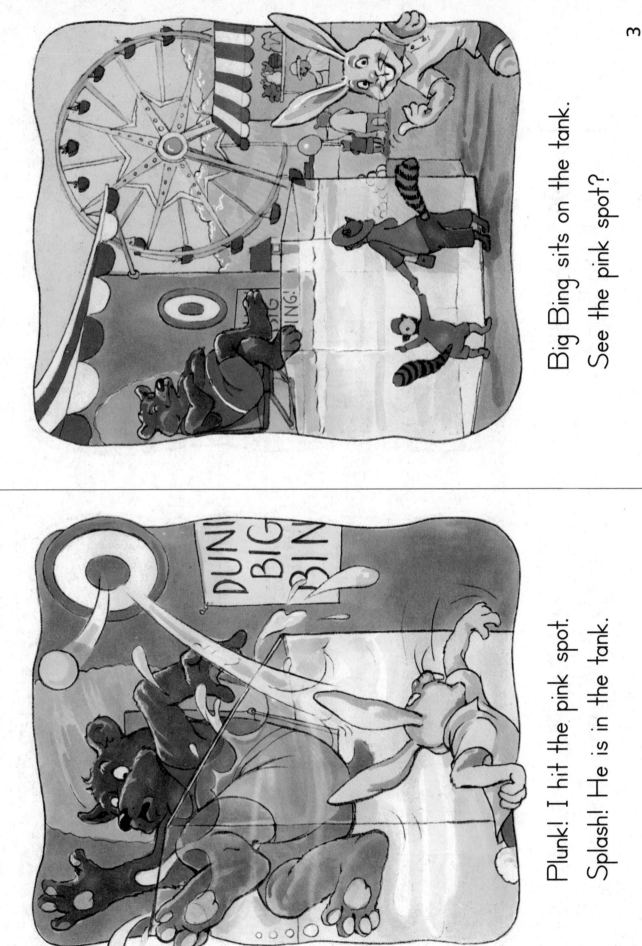

Big Bing sits on the tank.
See the pink spot?

Plunk! I hit the pink spot.
Splash! He is in the tank.

I can hit the pink spot.
I can dunk Big Bing.

Big Bing winks.
He thinks I can't dunk him.

Quick Quin

by David Nguyen
illustrated by Olivia Cole

Core Decodable 57

Mc Graw Hill Education

Bothell, WA • Chicago, IL • Columbus, OH • New York, NY

Did the liquid get on the quilt?

Not a drop got on the quilt!

8

2

Quin was quick.
She got her glass.

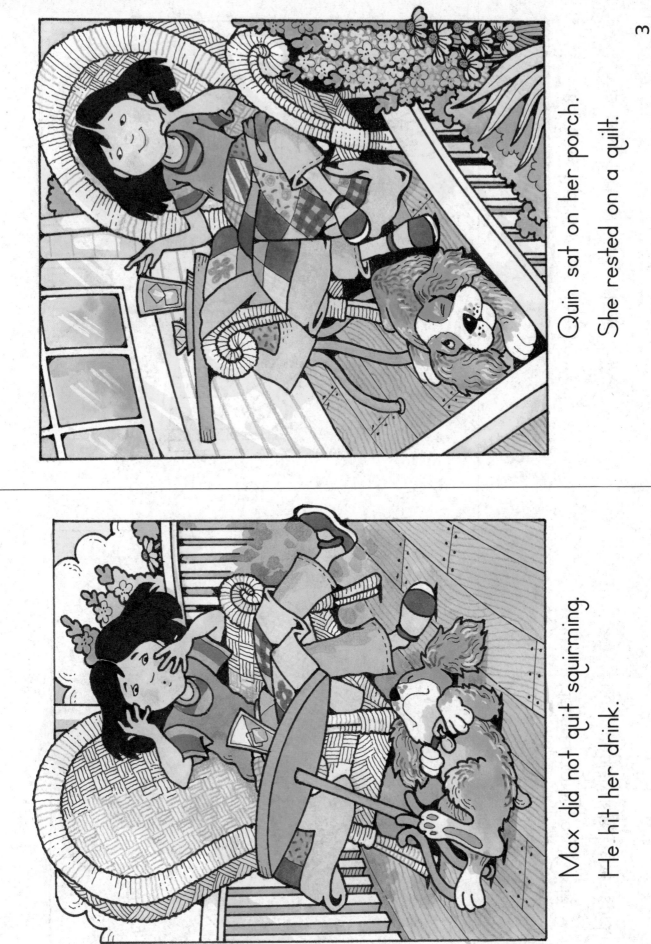

Quin sat on her porch.

She rested on a quilt.

3

Max did not quit squirming.

He hit her drink.

6

4

Quin was hot on her porch.
She squirted lemon in her drink.

Max was squirming on Quin.
"Quit squirming, Max," she said.

5

King Frank

by Ethan Cruz

illustrated by Benton Mahan

Core Decodable 58

Mc Graw Hill Education

Bothell, WA • Chicago, IL • Columbus, OH • New York, NY

Sir Quint grinned.

King Frank was not resting.

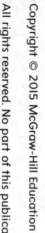

King Frank had a long shot!
Clank! He missed his shot.

15

271

King Frank rested.
He rested in the garden.

King Frank had a ball.
Bang! Bang! Bang!

Sir Quint hushed the men.
"King Frank must rest."

Sir Quint ran to the garden.
Bang! Bang! Bang! Clank!

Sir Quint hushed the kids.
"King Frank is resting."

5

Sir Quint did a bit of quick thinking.

12

Then a problem happened.
Bang! Bang! Bang! Clank!

6

"Quit clanking!" said Sir Quint.
But the kids did not clank.

11

274

275

"What is that banging and clanking?"
Sir Quint said, "That must stop this second!"

Bang! Bang! Bang! Clank!
Sir Quint ran to the kids.

Bang! Bang! Bang! Clank!
Sir Quint ran to the men.

"Quit banging!" said Sir Quint.
But the men did not bang.

Beth's Yak

by Betty Sanford
illustrated by Shawn McManus

Core Decodable 59

Mc Graw Hill Education

Bothell, WA • Chicago, IL • Columbus, OH • New York, NY

Is Beth's yak the best?

Beth thinks, "Yes!"

8

Beth sings to her yak.

Beth will not yell at her yak.

Beth had a big yak.
Beth kept her yak with her.

3

Beth has a yarn craft for her yak.

6

Beth kept her yak on her bed.
Beth kept her yak in her yard.

Beth fed her yak yams. Yum!
The yak did not have grass. Yuck!

Seven Pals

by Greg Frazier
illustrated by Jennifer Emery

Core Decodable 60

Bothell, WA • Chicago, IL • Columbus, OH • New York, NY

At ten, there were six best pals.

At eleven, there were seven!

8

2

All six pals talked.
Kevin talked.

7

Six pals met at ten.
All were best pals.

A kid was at the van.
The pals had never met him.
"I am Kevin," he said.

4

"A big van!" said Val.
All six pals spotted it.

Men were on the van's ramp.
"Let's visit that van," said Vick.

5

April's Bake Shop

by Lisa Boggs

illustrated by Yvette Banek

Core Decodable 61

Mc Graw Hill Education

Bothell, WA • Chicago, IL • Columbus, OH • New York, NY

Birds sit on top of her shop.

Birds ate her bread!

8

285

2

There is her table.
There is her plate.
What happened to her bread?

7

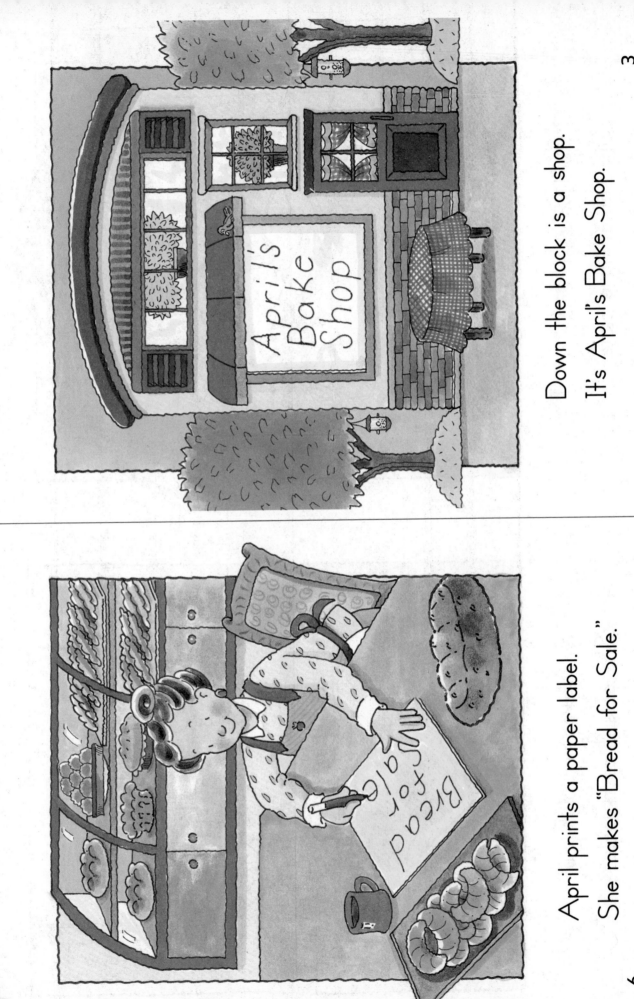

Down the block is a shop.
It's April's Bake Shop.

3

April prints a paper label.
She makes "Bread for Sale."

6

April bakes bread.
She sets it on a plate.

She takes her plate out.
She sets it on a table.

Tab

by Ethan Cruz

illustrated by Paige Keiser

Core Decodable 62

Mc Graw Hill Education

Bothell, WA • Chicago, IL • Columbus, OH • New York, NY

289

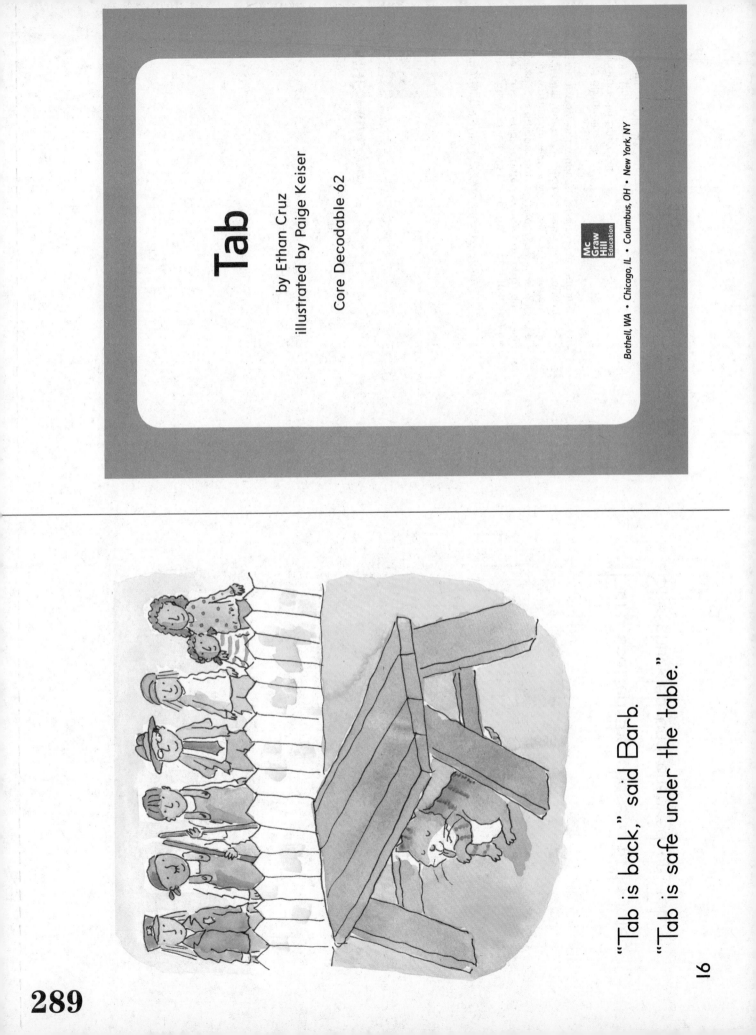

"Tab is back," said Barb.

"Tab is safe under the table."

16

Send all inquiries to:
McGraw-Hill Education
8787 Orion Place
Columbus, OH 43240

2

Barb spotted the chase a little later. She chuckled and checked on Tab.

15

290

Did the back gate shut?
Jane looked at the handle.

"This is a puzzle," said Jane.
"I cannot see Tab."

The gate did not shut.
Jane's kitten, Tab, left the yard.

4

Tab made a quick turn.
Jane did not see her.

13

293

Did Tab run fast?
Yes, quick Tab ran down Apple Lane.

5

"Stop, Tab!"
Kate and Jason yelled and helped.
Val and the men yelled and helped.

12

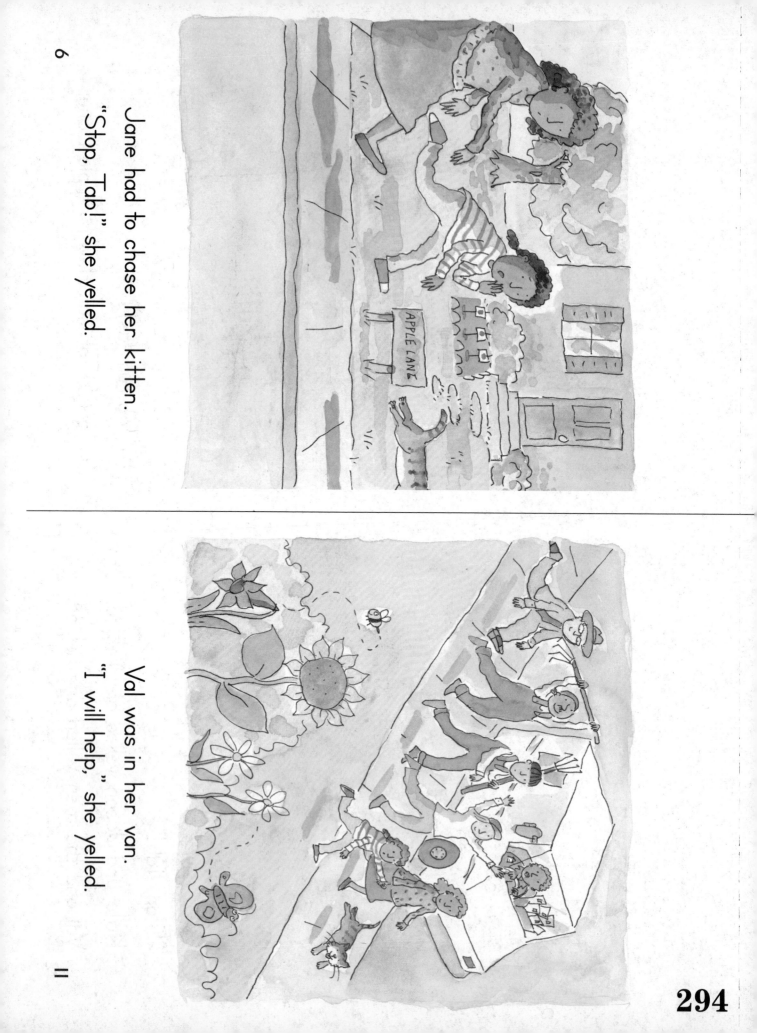

6

Jane had to chase her kitten.
"Stop, Tab!" she yelled.

Val was in her van.
"I will help," she yelled.

11

Kate set down her bottles.
"I will help," she said.

Little Tab ran and ran.

This game of chase was fun.

Tab ran past men with rakes.
The men helped and yelled, "Stop, Tab!"

Jason had seven bundles of paper.
"I can help!" he yelled.

9